ASSESSING TRAINER
EFFECTIVENESS

ASSESSING TRAINER EFFECTIVENESS

Leslie Rae

Gower

Published by
Gower Publishing Company Ltd
Gower House
Croft Road
Aldershot
Hants GU11 3HR
England

Gower Publishing Company
Old Post Road
Brookfield
Vermont 05036
USA

British Library Cataloguing in Publication Data
Rae, Leslie
Assessing trainer effectiveness.
I. Title
658.312404

ISBN 0 566 07264 5

Phototypeset by Intype, London
Printed in Great Britain by Clays Ltd., Bungay

Contents

Preface

If you're a training manager, how many times have you thought or even said to yourself:

'I think so-and-so (one of my trainers) is good, but
- How good?
- How good compared with others?
- How good should they be?
- How do I know?'

Similarly, if you're a trainer, whether you work in a commercial or industrial organization or in a dedicated training organization, or as a training consultant, have you asked the same questions of yourself?

I suspect that these questions have been asked many times in both situations, because the information is needed to ensure efficiency and effectiveness, and for development purposes. What's more, trainers as a 'breed' tend to be more self-critical and questioning than many other professions or occupations.

Having thought these question, what have you done about trying to obtain objective answers? On so many occasions the only action is to think:

Yes. He/she is a good trainer. I don't know how or why I say that (others say so), (he/she seems to get results), (the trainees seem to get on well with him/her), (etc.), I just know.

Fortunately these feelings can be correct, perhaps more often about somebody else than oneself, because we are consciously or subconsciously picking up various signals. When put together these signals produce the 'effective trainer' image in our mind – even though we are unable to say how we reached that conclusion.

How much more useful it would be to explore these factors in a more objective and analytical way. In some cases this approach is essential when people at a higher authority level say 'So you/he/she are/is a good trainer? Tell me how you *know*'. The answer 'I just know' is not acceptable. Perhaps you may feel the unacceptability of this response yourself without the demands of role boundary pressure. This book is intended to help trainers, and others concerned with the quality of training, to answer such questions as:

- What is an effective trainer?
- What are the skills of an effective trainer?
- Are we certain we are looking for the appropriate skills?
- What are the appropriate skills for my trainers/for me?
- What are the appropriate training skills for this industry/organization?
- How do I assess these skills and achievements?
- Are there standards with which I can compare my assessments?
- Which skills need to be developed – how and why?
- How can I maintain a control of these skill levels?

These questions certainly exercise (or should exercise) the minds of Training Directors, Training Managers, Trainers, Consultants and Line Managers. I have for some time managed trainer workshops for the Institute of Training and Development on this subject at which they have been raised; introduced a complete trainer assessment system into a large organization because they wanted answers to these questions; had the questions posed to me by individuals; and last but not least, asked them of myself!

We must not forget the other side of the equation – our clients are interested in the subject too. The line managers who are providing trainees want to know how skilled the trainer is and this information will help them in making their judgement on whether or where to send their people for training. Unless the manager has encountered the trainer previously, as a *trainee* or *learner*, on attending a training event, the questions in their mind may not be about the training itself, but

- What is the *trainer* going to be like?
- Will I like him/her?
- Will I be able to relate to him/her?
- Will I be able to learn from him/her?

Even though 'things' are necessary, people are more important than things.

The generic 'he', 'his', 'him' are used throughout the book for the sake of brevity and to avoid the ridiculous situations created by the use of plurals. Consequently, for 'he' also read 'she'.

Leslie Rae

1

The role of the trainer

For many years training was not recognized as a separate entity. New-comers to an occupation usually learned their 'trade' on the job, and 'Sitting with Nellie/Fred' was the most common form of introduction to the work. At worst they were told that 'x' was the best 'y' in the organization and if they watched them, they would quickly learn the job. In most cases 'x' was much more interested in getting on with the job, and thus earning money, than teaching someone else to do it. The 'learner' sat beside Nellie/Fred and watched, trying to make sense out of what was being done. Soon the manager/supervisor would declare that because the learner had seen what had to be done, they should now be able to do it. And so the newcomer was given his own work station and left to get on with it.

At the other end of the spectrum, we find a skilled and experienced worker, equipped by the organization with the skills of workforce training. This approach is exemplified in the well-known, although now defunct, TWI (Training Within Industry). It concentrated on the better aspects of the Nellie/Fred method of training by encouraging organizations to train their 'on the job trainers' in the skills of this method. Selected workers who had the job skills and the potential to learn to be trainers were taught the methods of job analysis, job instruction design and techniques, etc. 'Tell, Show, Do' are three words which became part of the training language as a result of this type of training. On the job trainers were given time to prepare for their training sessions and produce job training manuals or instruction sheets. Eventually these became the job training manuals now used by many industries. The newcomer was introduced to Nellie/Fred, who might describe the task and its functions, and show the learner the task in operation, at the same time describing what was happening and why. The learner, under the observation of the trainer, would then attempt either the task or parts of it, until it was obvious that they were capable of performing it to the required standard. The learner might then progress to the actual work, under strict supervision, and ideally in the early stages Nellie/Fred would monitor the results of their training.

The development of training

The change from 'sit down and learn' to the supported training by an on the job trainer required not only an improvement in training methods, but also a change in attitude to training. Whilst a newcomer was being trained in this more effective manner, the production that would have otherwise come from Nellie/Fred was lost. The employer was persuaded to accept this loss because it was now obvious that the newcomer would learn more quickly and more effectively and become an efficient producer themselves much more speedily. Because the learner was more efficient when starting production themselves, less waste would result. These changes therefore produced a decrease in costs, over a slightly longer term, in spite of the apparent short-term increase in cost.

The group approach in education had long been appreciated, but when the educational processes were transferred to training they continued as the didactic, sit and listen and learn approach. Courses consisted of either a series of lectures given by the trainers, or a similar series presented by guest speakers or visiting 'experts', who were experts in the subject, but not necessarily in the techniques of presentation. It was during this era that methods, albeit subjective and restricted, of assessing a trainer's skill were developed. As the trainer was only delivering lectures, or similar forms of input, these assessments were concerned with presentational skills.

This approach to training continued for many years, although one or two more enlightened trainers or organizations questioned its value and moved into more varied forms of training.

Research by educational and industrial psychologists started to show that the lecture form of training, where the learners sat passively and were expected to accept information and to be able to translate this into skills, was often not the most effective method.

Learning by doing

The training era of experiential learning, or learning by doing, was dawning and all the indications at that time were that if you did something instead of listening to people talk, you would return to work with some skill. The disillusioned trainers grasped this concept willingly, because many of them were as bored as their trainees with the interminable lectures. Training courses ceased to follow the traditional lecture form and became periods of intense activity, exercise and game playing. In many cases, this swing from the lecture to the game was extreme and soon it was realized that experiential training was not the panacea that it had appeared to be.

Most employers at this stage paid little attention to training and many were suspicious of its value. They had seen that their staff who had attended the lecture type of training had returned bored and uninterested and rarely put into practice anything they had learned. Now they saw them returning full of the games they had played and saying how enjoyable the experience had been, but little learning seemed to have taken place.

With a greater understanding of how people learn effectively came the realization that neither the lecture, nor the activity approach, nor many of the other alternatives were ineffective, people are different in the ways they learn, and because the trainee population is heterogeneous, the most effective form of training likely to suit the majority of this mixed population would be a training approach (not necessarily a course) with a varied content. This content would obviously not suit all the learners, all the time, but most would benefit greatly, some would at least learn something valuable.

Varied forms of learning

In addition to changes in the training approach training departments looked at the increasing number of other forms of learning aids available – films, videos, interactive videos, training packages, self-learning packages, computer-based and computer-assisted learning, etc. With these new methods learning through training should now be universal and more effective, and most subjective indications suggest that this is so, subjective because there is little real evidence about the limitations of the traditional methods and only limited objective evidence of the success of current approaches. Improvements do seem to be taking place however. As a result, individuals and organizations are starting to take training and development more seriously.

At the present time a trainer is required to be a person of high flexibility, knowledge and skills, able to introduce the most effective elements required by the situation.

Training and development

Two words have assumed much more importance in recent years – 'learning' and 'development'. The move from 'training' to 'learning' has accompanied the many changes in training methods. One of the principal changes has involved the change of emphasis in control of the learning event. With the trainer in the 'driving seat', the trainees had no option other than accept the directives of the trainer. The movement to a more participative mode of training means the transfer to the learners of some, if not all, control of the learning process, and in certain cases some of the content. Fears were expressed that this might produce a diminution in the material learned: in fact, in most cases, the learners demanded a more extensive range and depth of material.

For many, the ultimate type of learning is through the workshop, rather than the training course. In the workshop the learners decide to a large extent, within the agreed objectives, the content, extent and process of the workshop, sometimes the time necessary to process this learning, the actioning of the learning and its review and monitoring. The trainer's role changes radically: he becomes a resource for the learners, to be called upon to provide information, experiences, skill assistance, resources, support, etc. As this obviously demands the wider range of skills referred to earlier, the trainer ceases to be the traditional, 'presentational' type of trainer, which places more demands upon him than preparing his sessions/course within the limits of his knowledge and skills.

A change is required not only in the methods of trainer, or more correctly 'facilitator', but also in his attitude, for in giving up the reins he may also have to accept that he is not the universal expert – and does not need to be so. Experts, if required, can always be obtained from somewhere. There will, however, always be training needs which can only be tackled effectively in the more traditional way.

Development

'Development' is a word used widely and often loosely, sometimes as a synonym for 'training'. It has a wider meaning than training, which tends to be usually a singular learning activity, whether this is a training course, workshop, learning package, etc. Development can be considered as an overall approach to an individual's or group of individuals' improvement and enhancement. It can involve a series of training events of various types, preferably linked to lead to a total learning experience which leaves the learner stronger.

The advent of 'development' demonstrates yet another change to the attitudes which are applied to training. Originally training, like education, was looked upon as a series of isolated events which were themselves identified and developed in isolation and which produced a sum of knowledge and skills. In the developmental approach, each event is linked and relevant to every other event and to the total requirements of the learner and the organization.

The developmental aspect of training, with discussion on course content, demonstrates this desirable change in attitude and process. The need for discussion suggests that the trainer is not only much more involved in the training/learning with the learner, but also with another person with a responsibility in the process – the learner's manager.

The learning trinity

The line manager has always had the responsibility for the training and, particularly, the development of the staff. Traditionally, managers have regarded training as the province of the trainer because training was not 'work', and, after all, the trainers were the experts in training. In many cases, participants on training courses were there because they had been told to go and be trained, whether or not they wanted or needed it. The change of emphasis on development, rather than just training, requires a considered approach, and more involvement by line management. After all, the learners do not work for the trainers. They must train and develop to ensure that the job is carried out in the most effective way, which would benefit their immediate manager. In many cases, when a training/learning need arose at work, it was simple to send the person to a training course. In the mind of the line manager, this absolves them from doing anything themselves and allowed them to transfer the problem, albeit temporarily, to the trainer.

As training moves to a wider developmental structure, the need arises for an effective 'Training Trinity'. This trinity consists of the line manager, the trainer and the learner. The roles within the training trinity are generally quite well-defined, although there must be a certain amount of agreed overlap.

Line management
Although the skills of the trainer are an essential element in the training family, it is probably the active involvement of the line manager which is critical. The trainees are direct employees of the line manager and need his or her practical support:

• To determine individual, as opposed to corporate need;

- To encourage and actively support the satisfaction of needs, whether these have been identified by the individual or by the line manager;
- To ensure that the needs are met in the most appropriate manner and at the relevant time;
- To support actively the trainees on their return from or completion of the learning event; and
- To ensure that development is a continuing process rather than an isolated event.

Managers must be aware of the learning opportunities available, and work very closely with the trainer.

Once the initial decision has been made that training is required, with or without the early involvement of the trainer, the line manager can call on the trainer for a discussion about the ways in which the needs can be met, and agree with the trainer the most appropriate approach.

Before the training the line manager must conduct a pre-course briefing session with the learner to discuss the final details, agree training objectives for the individual and for the organization both local and corporate. At this stage the need for the training will be confirmed and the most relevant method agreed upon. Agreement is needed about a date on which the line manager and trainee will meet soon after the end of the training. Without such a meeting there is the danger that the learner will go away to the training in the belief that the manager has little or no interest in what is happening, that his absence from work is almost irrelevant, and there will be a similar lack of interest on his return.

Following the training, the line manager must meet again with the trainee in a post-course debriefing meeting. At this meeting they will discuss what has occurred during the training, what learning has been achieved, what action plans have been made, and to arrange future support and action. Again at this stage, the trainer can become involved for at least part of the discussion, particularly when the line manager may not be able to cope with the situation, or the problems may be too large for a non-expert to satisfy. The trainer should be there solely in a support role. The discussion should be between the manager and the trainee, and the trainer must resist either the temptation or the implied invitation to take over.

The trainer

Many of the trainer's activities within the trinity relationships are traditional ones, but he/she must become actively involved at an early stage in the discussion of training needs, who should be trained, when, in which specific areas, where, and so on. In the past it has been more common for the trainer to be told of these requirements and have to react accordingly.

In an ideal relationship, both the line manager and the trainer should work jointly to investigate into job and people requirements leading to training needs identification. The involvement of the line managers can be further developed if the trainer brings them into the stages of course objective development and also the broad construction of the training programme – the line manager brings the expertise of job knowledge, the trainer supplies the training and training programme expertise.

The line manager, if necessary with tuition by the trainer, can be brought into an active role on the training programme itself by being introduced into the programme as the expert on matters of the line; discussing 'real-life' management problems; raising such questions as what the line manager expects of his staff, and so on. Including 'real' line managers can often add credibility to a training programme.

In many organizations, the traditional role of the trainer stops when the training has been completed. In this partnership there should be much more of a continuing role. The debriefing activity by the line manager with the trainee has been stressed and, although this must remain the responsibility of the line manager, part of the debriefing action – advice on implementation, further or alternative learning, etc. – can be enhanced by the involvement of the trainer. The trainer may become actively involved in the continued learning at work, although this will depend on his/her availability. Care must be taken that the managerial responsibilities are not simply passed to the trainer to ease the manager's work, or because the manager simply does not wish to perform these duties.

Another potentially contentious issue in the discussion of roles is evaluation, the long-term assessment in cost-benefit terms of the training and training programmes. It can be argued that this is a continuation of the training event and the validation of that event and thus the responsibility of the trainer to follow through. The counter argument is that improvement in cost effectiveness occurs within the line operation and consequently the line manager is the one who should be responsible for carrying out the evaluation.

There can be no doubt that the line manager is in the most appropriate position to assess by observation and the analysis of production results the long-term success of the training and any improvements which may be the result of the training.

The most effective answer is a completely cooperative approach between the trainer and the line manager. A typical evaluation exercise could be follow-up questionnaires sent by the trainer to both the trainees and their line managers, followed by clarification and diagnostic interviews which will also serve the purpose of confirming both views. The line manager will be in a position to observe the trainee more closely. If a full practice of validation and evaluation has been followed, control groups will have been included in the evaluation programme. The trainer will be in a better position to maintain contact with these groups, whilst having constant contact with their line managers. By working together the trainer provides the expertise in training follow-up and the line manager the expertise in operational improvement assessment.

The trainee or learner

Last, but far from least, is the trainee without whom the whole exercise would have no value. In the past, very little notice has been taken of the wishes and needs of the learner, but if they are ignored and what is provided does not meet with their wishes, little learning will result and the training will have been a waste of time. We have seen so far that in so many ways each role-holder of the trinity participates at different stages of the learning process. The trainees must not be exceptions.

When the concept of the training is being formulated, the potential trainees are involved very much in activities related to the identification of the needs of the task, the level of competence of those performing the tasks or planned to perform the tasks – the determination of training needs. The ideal would be for the trainee to be directly involved in the planning of the training itself.

The changing role of training has already been considered, and the extent to which the emphasis of training/learning ownership is/should be passed to the learner is an important element in this change. Time is now often allocated at the start of the training event for the necessary planning to take place. In similar ways, the trainees can be involved in the validation of the event and the evaluation of the development programmes. Traditionally the pre-training event tests, the interim validation measures, the end-of-course validations and the long-term evaluation approaches were all constructed by the trainer or, on rare occasions, were a joint product of the trainer and line manager. These measures were then imposed on the trainee without question. More realistic and effective responses are likely if the trainees themselves are given a more prominent role in the decisions about these validation measures. For example, the trainees could be asked to produce the end-of-course questionnaire or method which they would find most acceptable and useful.

The training quintet

Important as these three role-holders may be, there are two other elements which must be taken into account if the training as a whole is to be completely effective. One of these, the Training Manager, is of considerable importance, and without the organization no training would be necessary. These two roles, added to the 'Training Trinity', produce the 'Training Quintet'.

Organization

The organization, usually senior management recognizes the need for training and sets guidelines to the training function, as statements of the developing needs of the organization. Developments in the medium and long term will suggest training needs.

The traditional approach, still all too common, has been to let the training section know when (and not until) the need arises. A more useful approach, particularly if the Training Quintet is to be of value, is for it to be organizational policy to bring training and development into discussions about the future developments at the earliest stages of discussion. In many cases this requires a change of attitude to training and development by senior management, who in the past have not taken training and development too seriously.

It should be obvious that given ample warning of changes ahead the training section can ensure that any action necessary is planned in good time, thus allowing it to be planned more effectively.

The training function is often too distant from senior management to have this effect. If the training role is to develop into a positive force in the organization, trainer attitudes must change so that the training department is recognized and accepted by senior management as a force which can help the organization in the achievement of its objectives. Much will depend on the hierarchical status of the trainer and it is in this area that the Training Manager, the fifth member of the Quintet, will be able to make a strong contribution.

The training manager

The Training Manager completes the quintet, although in some cases the trainer or Training Officer and the Training Manager are the same person. In many ways it is preferable if they have been Training Officers themselves at some stage – this is an extension of the classical argument about the need for a manager to be a subject expert. Perhaps more than the 'general' manager, specialist managers such as Training Managers will need to have a very good working knowledge of training and development. Often their role includes not only the management of the training function, but also specific training duties, perhaps with more senior managers. They will need to have a working knowledge of a wide range of training and learning methods, techniques and approaches, to aid them in the assessment of the trainers for whom they are responsible.

There are of course a number of different types of Training Manager, each with their own particular profile. At one extreme is the Training Manager who has no training staff at all, and, in addition to 'managing' the training function itself – planning, designing, negotiating, budgeting, etc. – will also be involved in direct training within the organization. These Managers are not rare and in many cases have to rely on external assistance to help them fulfil all the training demands made upon them. Usually they are found in small companies or small independent units of larger organizations. Their tasks can become very difficult to juggle – at the very time when they should be considering the development of the training function, and in particular its costing, they are more likely to be called away to perform a training task.

At the other extreme is the Training Manager who has almost exclusively a management role. He or she has a training team of several trainers, may be responsible for a learning resource centre, and also for negotiation and control of a training budget. Most of the work of this Manager is therefore in managing; but because of the specialism there is no excuse for their not having an extensive knowledge of training.

Within the training quintet the Training Manager has a very important and specific role. He will

- Agree training principles and programmes with the other members of the quintet;
- Support, in a managerial role, the trainer, ensuring that sufficient resources of whatever nature will be available;
- Participate in investigatory and research projects which will extend the range of learning facilities available;
- Negotiate during the early stages of a difficult liaison with line management to ensure that the quintet develops into a viable working unit.

Most important, the Training Manager is the link between line management and the trainer, representing the training viewpoint and, more particularly, the conceptual and functional needs of training and development with the top decision-making levels of the organization. Many are not in positions where they can wield reasonable power, but to ensure that the value of training in the organization is recognized and given the responsible position it deserves, a more pro-active approach must be taken by the Training Manager. On rare occasions only, the Training Manager, is invited to the first meetings of a working group, at whatever level in the organization, when new corporate projects are initiated. This early involvement ensures that potential training needs and activities are taken into account at this early stage.

The Training Manager is the linch-pin, having interest in all aspects of training and development, but also in co-ordinating the interests and requirements of the other members of the quintet.

It will therefore be seen that if a training quintet can be developed in an organization, then not only will the value of the Training Department be enhanced but training will be seen to be important. Senior management will look upon training as part of the strategic partnership, or at least a tactical arm of that strategic force. Line management, traditionally suspicious of the trainers, will, because they become so involved themselves, use training as a real part of their job and develop new working relationships. The learners will benefit and will cease to be pawns in the training *v* 'real world of work' chessboard. The trainers and the Training Manager will benefit because they will realize that their value is being recognized and that they have a place within the organization rather than being 'that lot in the training department'.

The assessment function in training

For these benefits to become a reality, the Training Manager must ensure that the training is performed to the best of the abilities of the trainers, that the learners actually acquire some learning, and, that, with the support of the line manager the learning is applied in the work place. These activities do not just happen unaided and the purpose of this book is to suggest the ways and means by which this may be achieved.

Part of the role of the Training Manager must be to maintain training standards at a high level (however these might be defined). A programme of assessment of both the training and the trainers will need to be initiated, enhanced or maintained, depending on the current circumstances. My experience suggests that, in the main, Training Managers assess their trainers *as and when they can* and *to the best of their abilities*. This usually means that from time to time – often at quite long intervals – the Training Manager sits-in on a session of one of his trainers, leaves without giving realistic feedback other than 'Uhh, that was OK, wasn't it?', and that is that. Such 'assessment' is not only unhelpful, it can be highly dangerous.

The Training Manager must be in frequent contact with, not only the trainers, but also the work of the trainers, for 1) the maintenance of high standards; 2) realistic feedback of performance to the trainers; and 3) support for the annual appraisal system. The first two reasons suggest a strict control and monitoring of standards, standards which have to be defined in the first place. How this is performed is the effective part of the action. It must not be, or be seen to be, inspectorial, and the model suggested later in this book should soften this effect although no degree of softening can take away the fact that an assessment of skill, efficiency and effectiveness is taking place.

The Training Manager or other manager responsible for the training function must obviously be the prime assessor in this activity, but my model suggests that a) this is done with agreement, and b) parallel assessments are performed by the trainers themselves, by their peers or co-trainers, by the trainees directly, and, in a more indirect way, by the training itself. Even if 'policing' is identified, much of this will be self-inflicted rather than externally imposed.

Link with appraisals

Where no trainer assessment system is in existence, the Training Manager, and hence the remainder of the organization, have no real measure of the skill of the training organization, and consequently are more likely to either assume the worst or accept any negative feedback they received from other sources. The Training Officers themselves can become frustrated by lack of feedback about their performance, and inter-relationships can become strained as suspicions arise.

An effective feedback system, however, can enhance not only the immediate feedback action, but also an annual appraisal system, if there is one in operation. Many appraisal systems rely on the once a year formal report and performance review interview. This interview can suddenly create ill-feelings between the two people involved as previously unexpressed criticisms are raised. The appraiser has obviously saved up all the bullets for this interview, perhaps under the impression that this was the occasion when they should be fired. 'Appraisals' of this nature can be traumatic and conflict-generating with the result that working relationships are harmed – 'Why didn't he say that when it happened instead of waiting until now!!'.

A planned and continuous feedback will ensure that there is at least the opportunity to make any comments – bad or good – nearer the time when the incidents occur. Immediate feedback will also allow early rectification of any faults by the trainer, rather than a repair operation following the trauma of the 'appraisal interview'. Although the approach suggested by Blanchard in *The One Minute Manager* may be rather on the sparse side, the basic approach of praise them or kick them *at the time* is very relevant.

Of course there are constraints. The more time the Training Manager allocates to trainer assessment, the trainer sits back to self-assess and others take to help in the assessment, the less time there is for other essential activities. There are communication tasks to be performed, administration to be kept efficient, negotiations with senior and line management to take place, reports to write, budgets to argue and maintain. The Training Manager's trainers are his *most important resource* – without them there is little reason to maintain a training department. Too often they are ignored for these administration reasons, knowingly or unknowingly, and sometimes because:

'I don't need to watch 'x' working, I know they're good and they don't need me to tell them'.

Often they may not know whether they are good or not, or how good they are as measured against the standards, and they *do* need to be told by their boss. Technical and professional managers tend to be even less effective at giving feedback:

'After all, my people (trainers) are technically trained/professionals so they do not need to be kept informed about how they are doing'.

Would that were so! In fact, in my experience professionals tend to be less sure of themselves than others and need reassurances. Structured yet friendly, formal yet natural feedback, may be given without an excessive use of precious time.

2

Trainer requirements

The previous chapter reviewed the role of the trainer and its relationship with others in general terms. But what is the basic role of the trainer; what is a trainer; what are they expected to do; are they all the same? These are but some of the many questions which must be answered before you can assess how well you or they are performing.

Training functions

The word 'trainer' carries a wide range of meanings, stemming initially from the function that the 'trainer' performs.

The workplace instructor
On the job instructors should be skilled, experienced and efficient operatives in the area of their normal employment. They must also possess:

- The interest and commitment to the development of other people (for the benefit of the organization was well as the individuals) to the extent that they will want to act as a trainer;
- An interest in helping other people to become proficient in a function of which they themselves may be proud; an innate ability or potential to learn to train, or a proven ability as a trainer.

Not all these interests or skills are evident without experience and practice and many people who have a strong desire to train, and firmly believe they can, are found wanting when it comes to the actual practice. Many examples of this can be seen, none more evident than the husband who decides/agrees to teach his wife to drive a car! The will is certainly there, and the driving experience and skill may also exist, and it may even be that his training skills have been proven in other areas, but because of the emotional factors involved, the normal skills of training do not seem to emerge and the training is a failure.

Emotions do not often interfere with straightforward face-to-face training at the workplace although other factors do have a similar effect. Often the 'Nellie/Fred' is casually given the job of training someone. Either the trainer, the learner or the boss quickly discovers that 'Nellie/Fred' is not a born trainer, or an innate ability emerges and a potential trainer is born. The far-sighted employer will recognize this potential and will make formal training facilities available for 'Nellie/Fred': the facilities of learning how to be a fully efficient and effective trainer or instructor.

The instructor

Mechanical, technical and procedural tasks require a straightforward approach in which the emphasis is usually on the teacher-taught environment. Although both the teachers and the learners may want to approach the learning event in a different, more 'enlightened' way, the training task demands that the subject is taught – at least in the earlier stages. Instructors in this environment must be highly self-disciplined and very knowledgeable about the subject, at least to the teaching level required and preferably beyond. They must have an up-to-date and valid brief, manual of instruction or procedural base from which to instruct; even a little variation from this approach is often impossible. In many cases, at least in the acquisition of knowledge, the instructor can be replaced by an artificial instructor in the form of a computer, video, audio cassette, manual or 'noddy' book. In these cases a live instructor may be preferable, even if only to support the open learning approach. When it comes to the practice of applying the knowledge, in most cases the services of an instructor are necessary.

Particular types of trainers will make good instructors. The worst type of trainer for this role will be the one who insists on saying always 'Why do we do it like this?', 'I would like to try something out. It may not work, but it will be a variation', etc. However, this attitude must be applied initially, or at some stage, to the instruction to ensure that challenges to the system have not been made, or are rejected, because of apathy, hidebound tradition, instructor preferences and corporate politics. If the approved method is really known to be the most appropriate, questioning or the questioner has a high nuisance value.

Although group instruction has existed for a long time, its use became widespread during the Second World War when many unskilled men and women had to be taught quickly the basic elements of jobs needed for the war effort. In order to help the induction, the training for these tasks were often broken down into smaller parts which could be learned in sequence. The formal instructional method known as TWI (Training Within Industry) also developed during this era. Because there were so many people who had to be trained in this way, group instruction methods developed.

The mechanistic approach to training need not be without its lighter side to break the formality. On one occasion an expert instructor was due to give an introductory session on the safe handling of explosives. He was only a few minutes into his session when, from the back of the room, came a small but distinct explosion. Pandemonium ensued among the learners for a while, but when the instructor was able to quieten them down he was able to tell them that it had been a planned explosion with 'x' pounds of explosives. He then invited them, many of whom had never experienced an explosion previously, to imagine the explosion with x^n pounds of explosives, the more usual charge. Learners gained more from this experience than from a film.

In another incident, a colleague of mine was required to tutor a training session on the Social Security Regulations relating to Share Fishermen, a complicated, dull subject about statistics, etc. This trainer was a very ebullient person and, after two extremely boring sessions, both for him and the learners, he decided to try something to lighten at least part of the session. Thirty seconds after the session was due to start he burst open the door and strode in wearing wellingtons, oilskins, so'wester and carrying a fishing rod from which dangled half a plastic fish. A colleague threw half a bucket of water at him from outside in the corridor. Standing there in that outlandish garb, dripping with water and with the ridiculous fish dangling in front of him, he announced 'I've come to talk to you about Share Fishermen!' The group exploded with laughter, but when they had settled down somewhat, even though he conducted the session very much as previously, the atmosphere was quite different and the learning vastly improved.

The trainer/tutor

This is probably the largest category of trainer and will almost certainly remain so. Trainer/tutors are required to have wide knowledge of techniques, approaches and methods. The principal activity is the presentation of training sessions, with or without the use of a range of visual aids, linking the lecture with discussion or other activities. Other skills are those of discussion leading, setting, controlling and debriefing role-plays, activities and case studies; showing films and videos and linking these with associated activities; controlling and supporting training packages, computer program and other supported learning systems, etc. Often, the trainer designs the learning events and stays in control of most of the situation. He/she is the foundation of the large training department which relies on formal, structured training to satisfy the large scale demands of the corporate population.

The facilitator

As we saw in the previous chapter, training is increasingly moving away from the formal training course to events which are initially trainer-designed and led, but which quickly develop into workshops in which the learners are given more and more control of the event. In such cases, the 'trainer' needs to have all the knowledge and skills of the 'trainer/tutor', but may need to be even more knowledgeable in view of the unforeseen demands which might be made by the learners. So the available toolkit must be bulging with roles, cases, activities, subject scenarios and mini-sessions of a wide range. Above all, the facilitator must be able to stand back and not present himself as the expert, rather a resource, albeit a very skilled one, for the free use of the learners. He must be able to intervene or stay remote at the appropriate moments; to lead (with all the different meanings to the word); to offer relevant activities, but then allow the learners to progress or regress, not intervening, but allowing them to dig themselves out of the holes they have dug for themselves.

As the organizations change their approaches to training and development from traditionally-run courses to more human resource-related approaches, the existing 'trainers' need to develop into this wider role of the Facilitator. Many can make this transition, but there will always be some who are unable to let go of the controlling reins. There is obviously a place for these in certain types of training and organizations.

The consultant/adviser

Until relatively recently the corporate demand for wide and educated consultancy and advice was satisfied almost exclusively by external agencies, comprising private consultants with a wide range of experience in industries and companies. The internal trainers, although experts in their own fields, did not always have the knowledge and skills necessary to offer wide-ranging advice. There has been an increasing demand in many organizations, particularly the larger ones, to have their own internal consultants. It was found beneficial for the internal agents with the extensive knowledge of the internal working of the organization, its politics, its culture, its procedures and its needs to be given the resources and time to extend their knowledge. The disadvantage is the danger that, an internal consultant might be too inward looking.

The internal consultants, if they have corporate credibility, can tackle the wider company needs through extensive, but inexpensive, training needs analyses; become involved in more individual tutorials or advice with senior management; search for, and advise on, wider developmental opportunities, including those in the educational field; become the repository of an extensive 'library' of information and views about training and development methods, centres of excellence which can be recommended; advise on appropriate avenues of learning, etc.

It may be inappropriate to introduce hierarchies amongst trainers, but this happens. Some try to equate the status or skill level of operative, supervisor and management training with 'trainer levels'. I feel this is an unhelpful approach because all forms of training require different, not necessarily better skills for the various groups. There does seem to be some advantage, however, in considering the skill hierarchy of the Instructor and the Trainer (if these two are differentiated because of training need rather than skill or attitude), then the Facilitator, and the Consultant/Advisor. This is because the three types need to acquire skill, knowledge, techniques and attitudes in order to progress from one position to the other. There will always be exceptions who can enter one or other level without having experienced the skills of the preceding one, but successful practitioners of this nature are rare.

The Trainer of Trainers

This specialist group of trainers is found in organizations with relatively large training departments, or in specialist training organizations such as BACIE (British Association for Commercial and Industrial Education), the Industrial Society, the Institute of Training and Development, in the USA the American Society for Training and Development, and other more commercially based trainer training companies.

The basic problem is similar to that discussed earlier concerning the skill needed by managers: to what extent does the Trainer of Trainers need to have served an apprenticeship as a trainer before being allowed to teach trainers? Does the Trainer of Trainers need to have been highly skilled and effective as a trainer? Or does one have to accept the derogatory suggestion, often quoted – 'If you can't do it, teach it!'.

The recruit to trainer training should be one of the most effective, skilled and experienced practising trainers possible. Only trainers with this skill level have the credibility and the experience on which to draw and introduce into their training to make it widely applicable.

Otherwise the role of the Trainer of Trainers is very similar to that of the general trainer or facilitator, but with the ability to relate closely to the role of their learners, and of course vice versa. Deliberately or not, desirable or not, they are presenting themselves as role models before the embryonic trainers. If they are seen to be performing in a particular way, some of the learners will copy this practice. If the performance is an appropriate one, this is not unacceptable but otherwise serious damage can be done. It is for this reason that the training team must be carefully selected, where possible. In the training team I managed, I had the extrovert, boisterous, activist type of trainer; the serious, logical, well-prepared, fairly staid but absolutely reliable trainer; and the highly skilled, articulate and 'clever' trainer with strong facilitator tendencies. These three, the basic team, complemented each

19

other, but also offered three of the possible role models for the learners to see in action.

The training designer

In recent years the role of the training designer has developed and become a force which is strongly allied to classical training.

Training events are ceasing to be isolated events and are becoming complete packages, linking throughout the event and also with other training approaches. It is the Training Designer who identifies and analyses the needs of the learners and trainers and designs a total package. This might consist of a set of instructional briefs or a manual, with all the necessary master OHP slides, a video and accompanying trainers' and learners' handbooks, perhaps an audio cassette, all the required handouts either in collated sheet form or as a comprehensive booklet, and a trainer's guide to the whole package. The package is then tested and produced and made available as an 'off the shelf' pack for trainers.

Not all training requirements in different organizations or different parts of one organization will require the same approach however, and in such cases the specific package can be too directive in content and method. On the positive side, if the operating trainer is inexperienced, the structure given supports his lack of experience and eases his entry into training. The more experienced trainer will be able to manipulate much of the provided material to suit his requirements. If time is limited and the trainer is not able to sit down and design his own training – and this can take a substantial amount of time – all or much of his material is presented in the package, in addition to providing the methods of presentation.

The role of the 'non-training trainer' can be compared with that of the consultant/manager of an internal resource centre. This is a facility which is more than just a library although it does contain books in the range of supervisory, management and professional/technical knowledge and skills. It also contains the widest possible range of films, videos, interactive videos, audio packages, computer programs, training packages, games, activities, role plays, etc. Access to this valuable collection of physical resources can be made easier by the linked consultant (who may also be the manager of the resource centre), who can guide the user of the centre to the most appropriate resource. Few resource centres are as well equipped as this, because the range of resources is so wide that a complete centre would be a very substantial one. It not only has to provide the 'software' resources, but also any 'hardware' necessary to use the resources – banks of computers, IV players, audio equipment, video playing equipment, etc. Most centres have to make do with the maximum amount of resources available within their allocated budget, and therefore a greater emphasis is placed on the skill and knowledge of the consultant/manager, who should be aware of where other available resources are located. A mammoth task.

Several organizations have attempted to make parts of this information available: for example, the *National Training Index*, a textual publication which attempts to list all or most of the organizations involved in training and what they can provide; MARIS which attempts the same listing, but as a telephone line linked computer database of open learning material; and other aids including TAP, a simply operated computer access point, available to the public, which details information about local or national sources of further or higher education or vocational training. TAP is administered by the Training, Education and Enterprise Division of the Department of Employment (formerly the Training Agency).

Some organizations have attempted to bring all this together. When I was employed as an internal consultant with the Training Agency, I initiated a project aimed at detailing on a computer database all the training courses offered by all the training providers external to the Agency and summarizing information about each one. This would link with the in-house learning resource centre, and the other sources of different information, MARIS, OPTIS, etc., to provide a complete (as possible) source of training information in Britain. The program was to be made as simple as possible, so that enquirers would only need to press a key to obtain whatever information they required. If wider information was required, resources would be at hand to help them with the communication links to the other sources.

This became a 'Forth Bridge' type of project which was still incomplete when I left the Training Agency 18 months later, as a result of a number of staff and staffing resource problems. Before all the selected details were entered about the training providers for whom there was information held, new information was flooding in which made amendment necessary to most of the entries! And so it continued.

The largest problem was not quantity of information, although this was a serious hurdle, but quality advice. If, for example, a learner asked for information on time management training, it was relatively simple to provide a list of books, videos, audio cassettes, computer interactive videos and training courses which were available (or at least those which had been entered into the program) – a substantial amount of material. The next question would be 'Which is the best?' or 'Which course should I follow?'. In order to answer this question effectively, the resource consultant would need to know the value-effectiveness of each of the resources available, plus an evaluation of the learner's preferred or possible learning style. This was an almost if not completely impossible task, which meant that the resource capability, however extensive, could never provide total advice.

One way of looking at this problem would be to consider that even though the resource information was not complete, it was more extensive (better?) than anything previously existing, and this would be so in most cases.

No doubt there are other trainer roles of this nature, and of course many trainers act in a multi-role situation, either consecutively or concurrently. In the context of effectiveness it is necessary to identify, certainly from the Training Manager's point of view, which type(s) of trainer you require, and from the trainer's point of view which type you need to be and/or want to be. There is little value in a trainer objecting to criticism or self-criticism of his skill as an instructor if all his energies are being directed at being a facilitator (and the organization wants an instructor). As a first step in the approach to the assessment of trainer effectiveness, the overall role or roles which need to be fulfilled must be defined. If you are the Training Manager, ensure that this role is the one you

- Want
- Are assessing.

The very skilled trainer will be able to cover all the roles as need arises, although some are so different it is not just a question of skill, rather one of attitude. A Training Manager, who is also a direct trainer and offers a number of facilitator demands events, told me recently that he was actually incapable of taking on the role of an instructor in its most restrictive sense. He had tried this and when he had to lead a very specific procedural session in which he was regarded as the oracle, saying 'This is what you do', he found that within a short period of time he would be moving into his facilitator role and saying 'This is what you *ought* to do. How do you feel about that?'. His move from the required highly directive, instructive role to a more natural reflective, flexible one was quite inappropriate in these circumstances.

The training manager

Although the effective trainer will continually engage himself in self-assessment, much of this assessment will be performed by the Training Manager. What is a Training Manager? A simple definition is that a Training *Manager* is a manager who is in charge of the training function. If only it were as straightforward as that! It has been mentioned earlier that a Training Manager can take on a variety of roles: a Training Manager with no staff, a Training Manager, Training Officer and Administrative staff all rolled into one; through the Training Manager with no staff but who contracts out all his training to external providers and consequently is almost completely an Administrative Manager; to the Training Manager with no personal training involvement but with a team of trainers and administrators, a manager in all senses of the word.

The culture and needs of the organization will determine the roles to a large extent for the Training Manager, much as he determines those of the Training Officers. Some variations are possible in addition to those imposed by the organization, although even these will be constrained in some other way – time, resources, etc. As a Training Manager with eventually a substantial but not overloaded (at that time) team of trainers, I was at one time charged with developing a management training structure with an organization which was in a high state of change and in which the prior management training had been minimal and largely ineffective (I had experienced this at first hand as one of the managers!)

My early role on taking up this post was that of consultant, involved in the diagnosis and analysis of training needs and presenting this analysis in the form of recommendations for acceptance by the organization. The approach recommended and eventually agreed upon suggested a change from a type of management training event which included just about everything and taught little, to a series of knowledge and skills modules. These modules did not exist in any form at that stage, so my first role change was to become a training course module designer assisted by a small group of Training Officers. Once designed, the modules were gradually introduced and, usually in the early stages, I acted with one of the Training Officers as a Training Officer myself on the new modules, whilst continuing the design role and also taking on an increasing management role. Once the earlier modules had been introduced and were on their way to becoming established, I withdrew from the direct training role and injected in my place another trainer who had been recruited and trained in the meantime. So again I was back to a strong management role with the team of trainers performing the training functions on my behalf. I did, however, maintain an element of direct training in one or two modules where my particular skills were necessary and appropriate and where further diagnoses were necessary, not only of subjects required, but also of the potential trainee population.

Finally, with a full complement of trainers (in addition to a capability to engage external consultants on contract) I was virtually a manager pure and simple, although I still indulged in some of the training activities which appealed to me!

This arrangement is not an uncommon one and it meant that I covered many of the roles in which many Training Managers find themselves more or less permanently involved.

As a Training Manager of whatever nature, the questions which arise in the assessment of trainer effectiveness, apart from those directly related to the trainer skill, are concerned with attitudes. Is the trainer operating in the general role required by the organization? Is the trainer seen as committed to the required role? Is the Training Manager himself in tune with what is required by the organization? Does the Training Manager *know* which role he is in fact playing?

23

Assessment of trainer effectiveness involves not only the examination of the trainer's *skills* by the Training Manager and the Training Officers themselves (and as we shall see, by others in addition to the two principles), but a questioning of the value of each general role within the organization. Assessment all too often takes account of the skill aspect only.

The descriptions of the various trainer roles demonstrates the care necessary in allocating a title to a 'trainer' or training function. Even the role descriptions given here are not universally applied – for example, 'trainer' is often seen as identical to 'instructor'. When assessment is involved, however, it is the role, not the title, that should be recognized and understood.

3

The skills of the effective trainer

Although other factors are important, it is the trainer skill which is in question. What are these skills which must be considered in assessing the overall capability of the trainer? Burgoyne and Stuart (*Personnel Review*, Vol 5, No 4, 1976) produced a list of what they considered to be the skills required for a management trainer. The following description of trainer skills is based on this list, amended on the basis of my own research with groups of trainers from all sorts of disciplines and organizations, and naturally supplemented from my experience as a developing trainer.

Organizational knowledge

Knowledge about the organization or company will vary according to whether we are considering an internally or externally-based trainer. The internal trainer must be very aware of the organization/company role and products or service, the policies which dictate the day-to-day operation and the developing projects. He/she must know the power structure within the organization, and from that the potential power of the people under training – how powerful are they, where are they placed in the hierarchy and where are they likely to go, what is their potential power, etc.? The vast majority of organizations have either internally developed and enforced procedures and rules, and/or externally enforced regulations, e.g. Health and Safety Regulations. These and any other functional procedures must be known by the trainer, perhaps not necessarily in detail, but sufficiently so that the training messages do not conflict with what *has* to be. Many training recommendations concern the deployment and use of resources and people. Credibility can be lost if the trainer recommends and tries to insist on practices which are completely inconsistent with the availability of these resources.

The external training provider, who is equally a contender for effectiveness assessment by the client, is in a more difficult position. He or she may not be in a position to know or even find out in advance of the training about essential information. It is so vital to the success of any effective provision of training, that every attempt must be made both before *and during* the event to obtain as much information as possible. Real skill is often necessary to obtain this information during the event, whilst training is proceeding. The apparent skill and credibility of the provider are reduced each time a lack of knowledge becomes apparent. If this is so for the external provider, how much more important for the internal trainer.

Management roles and functions

A further element of knowledge, linked with the previous skill, is that concerned with the extent of the managerial role in the organization. What is the range of the manager's role, what are the extents and limits of responsibility and authority? What are the lines of reporting and what levels of resources are available to them? Has a particular management role in the company any differences from similar role titles in other departments, parts of the company or other organizations? How free are managers to develop their organizational roles or do a number of constraints operate which can have an effect on a desire to change? Is there a 'Management Image' in the company and to what extent do the managers in the training population fit this image?

Training knowledge

Training knowledge must include familiarization with the academic and theoretical models and concepts applicable to training. The trainer must have a wide knowledge of the range of training techniques, methods and approaches in order to put these models into practice, and a good appreciation of the circumstances in which each is the most appropriate. As discussed in the previous section, the various 'trainer roles must be understood and the trainer must be able to identify the appropriate one for a particular situation. Many training authorities expect the trainer to know not only the details of a model, but also the 'originators' or developers of the model. Knowledge of models is sometimes looked on as an end in itself, rather than the means to trace back to what the originator really meant. Note that I do not use the word 'inventor', because there is little in training which is invented: most is developed from other practices or commonsense applications.

Programme preparation skills

Most trainers, at some stage or other in their careers, have to consider, design and prepare a complete training programme which will satisfy the identified needs of the organization or individuals/groups within the organization. Programme preparation requires skills in drawing together the material necessary for the event, selecting the most appropriate, putting it into a coherent, logical and progressive order, and arranging its presentation in manageable sessions. Decisions have to be made on the most appropriate way in which different parts of the content may be best presented – an input presentation session, a discussion, a role play or activity, use of a video, IV, or a computer program. Other decisions include those about whether parts of the programme would be more effectively dealt with outside the event in an open learning approach or as a self-learning package, etc. Many training contents can be approached in a number of ways, and a skill element of the designing is the decision about the most effective approach taking into account the training population, the subject, the remainder of the event, the skills of the trainers, etc.

Sensitivity to programme feedback

Too many trainers who present the programme they have designed or had designed for them are oblivious to the reaction of the learners as the event is proceeding. It is essential for the trainer to remain aware throughout the event, being sensitive to the behaviour and direct or indirect feedback from the learners. It may be necessary for specific activities to be included to encourage this feedback to occur, for often a group may have strong feelings about the training or the trainer but is unwilling or unable to feed these feelings back to the trainer. For example, when I run a week-long Interpersonal Skills Course, at the start of the 3rd, 4th and 5th days I offer a Feelings Review which allows a continuous check on the delegates' attitudes. I invite the delegates to write down, then share and discuss as openly as possible, three words which express their feelings at that point. This can often serve as a release valve for some pent-up feelings and the discussion can be traumatic. As with any solicited feedback, the trainer must be willing and able to accept this feedback and deal with whatever problems might emerge.

People skills

The principal skill of a trainer is not the ability to accumulate knowledge, but to communicate this knowledge to other people. He/she must ensure that the information is understood, remembered by the trainees and that they are capable of both acting on the information and recall. Whatever the personality of the trainer, his behaviour must be helpful to the learners. If the behaviour is such that the learners take a dislike to the trainer, the material presented must be really powerful to overcome this antipathy, which may affect the training.

A wide variety of people skills is required, because in modern training situations it is necessary for a full range to be employed. When delivering an input session, the skills of effective presentation are to the forefront, linked with an awareness of verbal and non-verbal signals which inform the trainer of the extent to which the material is being received. When input is linked with discussion and questioning, the additional skills of presenting 'good' questions, listening to the responses, encouraging contributions and probing to ensure understanding and emergence of views, also come into play. In group activity the trainer must be capable of dealing with a number of different people at the same time, of allowing them to interact without interruption, and of knowing when and how to intervene using an appropriate type of intervention. Again, when using games, exercises, role plays and activities, other skills are used or added to some of the others so far mentioned. The trainer must be skilled in presenting the activity information, content or process and must be able to leave the groups alone when they are taking part (even if they are going wrong), and certainly have strong skills of eliciting feedback after the events.

The trainer, particularly the new trainer, must always remember that he is in a position of power. The trainer is frequently unaware or forgets this. I have often been surprised some way into a training event when comments or statements which I have made much earlier in the event are quoted back at me – 'On x day at y o'clock, you said . . .'! From this power position there is an opportunity to influence, and this must be used for the benefit of the learners, even to the extent that it can sometimes be used deliberately to model or encourage certain attitudes or behaviours.

The temptation to play games with people who are in a less powerful position than the trainer can sometimes be overwhelming. But this feeling *must* be resisted, because apart from being morally wrong, a backfire can easily occur when the learners realize what is being done to them. Remember that behaviour, the most powerful human attribute in dealing with others, breeds behaviour – what you do to me, I will do to you!

Resilience

The trainer's function is not to influence people by making friends; training is not a popularity contest. Some trainers become upset if they do not become one of, if not the most popular of figures in the group and employ all sorts of tactics to ensure that this happens, even if the behaviour is not congruent with the needs of the training. If the trainer concentrates on the training and the needs of the learner, there will be occasions when the trainer is far from popular; he must be capable of dealing with this, particularly if the 'unpopularity' has been fostered for the sake of the learning. In many facilitative situations, the trainer who will be acting as an observer will see the group perhaps digging holes for itself, following false trails, allowing itself to be dominated by one of the members, etc. The temptation can be strong to help them and get them out of their difficulties (and at the same time receive their gratitude): this is usually the completely wrong course of action, because there is the need for the group to learn to solve its own problems.

Stress is not the prerogative of the learners who imagine (they tell me!) that the trainers are superhuman and can cope with whatever is thrown at them. On the contrary, if the trainer is concerned about the success of his training, he will be under even more stress than the learners – he will have the problem of the stress of the situation itself, as well as the stress of not letting this show to the learners. Of course, there will also be the situations when it may be advisable for the trainer to let his stress emerge in view of the group – yet another decision skill!

When the trainer has to play a role or roles that are foreign to them, they are put under a different kind of pressure, which again they may not show. All these and other situations make the role of the trainer particularly difficult because they are supplementary to the normal pressure of being in the training position. Faced with these stresses, the trainer must have emotional and behavioural resilience as he is often not in a position to deal immediately with the internal stress.

Commitment

Commitment to the training and development of other people, to the organization to ensure that it is performed effectively, to producing learning events at the most effective level, and to developing themselves to a stage when these other activities are possible, is essential for the trainer. Without commitment the training will suffer in a myriad ways. The absence of enthusiasm and sincerity to 'sell' a new idea or method will very quickly be realized by the learners and will reflect in their reactions. Learners excuse many faults and failings in their trainers when they recognize their enthusiasm, interest and commitment, but the reverse also applies.

The organization must not expect this commitment as a right. Many trainers are appointed within an organization when they have never considered this move previously as part of their career, and can become a 'trainer' with no initial enthusiasm. The commitment and enthusiasm of many fellow trainers, and the intrinsic interest and excitement of training often changes the attitudes of these initial non-believers. Not all are affected in this way however, and for those every day of training must be a pain or a terror. Not everyone is interested in, nor indeed capable of, training, and if this shows, and it surely will, the quicker the individual is out of training the better for themselves, their clients, the organization, etc.

Mental agility

Training, particularly at the present time, is a lively, active and constantly changing area. Although little in the way of techniques and methods is new, the methods of presentation and production are always developing – or at least changing. To learn all the techniques and methods, and to keep up with developments to the extent of being able to use them in an appropriate and effective way, requires an enquiring and agile mind.

The days of the training lecture session in which the trainer controlled completely the content, level and extent of the material are over, apart from perhaps the strictly procedural forms of training. The trainer has to be ready and able to answer penetrating and advanced questions drawing upon a sound knowledge. One of the ways in which credibility is lost so easily is the over-use of having to say that you do not know the answer, will find out and report back. Of course, this must happen on occasions – you cannot know everything – but when it becomes the norm, there is something wrong.

Creativity

Modern training, as we have seen, is not the presentation of what has always been presented and in the way it has always appeared – 'This subject has always been taught from a lecture, so'. The effective trainer must constantly be seeking new and realistic material, different ways of conveying information, not just for the sake of difference, but also for increased effectiveness.

These demands require the trainer to be constantly aware of what is happening elsewhere and to consider how these other approaches, etc. can be used, modified or not, in the existing training. Awareness of a variety of training techniques and methods will almost certainly spark off, if not original ideas, different ways in which a feature can be improved. Creativity is necessary and to be applauded, but there is also nothing wrong in taking existing approaches and changing them for your own purposes, particularly if the 'new' way is an improvement on the old.

As an example of this type of modification, two particular activities are described in *50 Activities for Developing Management Skills*, Volume One (Leslie Rae, Gower, 1988). Both these activities are modifications of 'The Report Activity'. In one variation, a group activity which is designed to demonstrate planning, behaviour planning, effective group working, negotiation, conflict handling, etc. has three basic steps.

1. The production, in two separate groups, of a report comparing two opposing activities or points of view, e.g. group versus individual problem solving.
2. A planning period in which each group plans its strategy, as a group and individuals, how to perform the one-to-one negotiations which will form the third stage.
3. The third stage in which each individual from a group meets face to face with an individual from the other group to negotiate the allocation of points between the two reports.

Alternatively, the third stage may be replaced by a joint meeting of the two groups to allocate the points between the reports. In both cases there is a fourth stage which is the feedback and discussion of the task results and processes which led to these. Both these activities are susceptible to a number of variations of attitude, timing, etc., but on one occasion I produced a third variant which I have found to be very effective. I was working in an area of change and needed to provide an activity which included this factor. There was no time to produce a custom-built activity, so both the 'Report' variations were used – with a twist. The groups were started on the first stage with the information that they would eventually be engaging in the one-to-one negotiations. About two-thirds of the way through the first stage, two members from each group were exchanged – a first element of change. During the second stage, with about five minutes to go before the negotiations were due to commence, the groups were told that individual face-to-face meetings were not possible, so they would have to meet as one group – a second element of change. In many cases changes introduce aspects of conflict and provide considerable material for discussion.

Self-development

Hand in hand with many of the other skills come the ability and the commitment to improve one's own skills in a self-developmental programme. It is so often easy to plan, advise on, inform and process the development of others, but much more difficult when you have to do this for yourself. This process involves both knowledge and skill, and is essential for the trainer in keeping up to date, abreast of training developments, and ensure development within the profession.

In company with most occupations and professions, training and trainers cannot stand still. If they try to do so, consciously or subconsciously, they are likely to egress. Although there is little 'new' in training, trainers must keep up to date with the developments of the existing material, different ways of using it, and so on. Also, of course, they must be aware of and able to learn about new products – films, videos, computer programs, interactive video, equipment such as black whiteboards, automatic printing whiteboards, OHP slide producers, etc.

The knowledge content includes self-awareness of your own behaviour and its effects, so that you might engage in a programme of behaviour modification to improve your training effectiveness.

If you are engaged in one form of training, but there are others in your organization and these are considered as important for career progression, it is in your interests to learn more about these other areas and so increase the size of your personal trainer's toolkit.

If training, as so often happens, is looked upon as a useful stage in the progression of a career-minded person, you will need to find out how long the period in training is optimum from a career point of view, and ensure that you have the necessary qualifications or knowledge to move *up* when your time to move *on* arrives.

One of the indicators of future success is the desire to develop to the fullest extent possible, even if this means self-activity. An intent self-developer will almost certainly be a high achiever at any stage of their progressive career.

Self-awareness

The uninterested trainer will usually be seen as ineffective. If an individual trainer has either no skill or no interest in their own effectiveness, they could be doing considerable training damage. However, the trainer who keeps on asking himself and others 'How am I doing?' will have a much greater opportunity of determining their effectiveness, and whether and what they need to improve.

As in any aspect of work, feedback to others on their behaviour and performance and general communication will trigger the behaviour-breeds-behaviour syndrome, and will prompt a return feedback of information.

Self-awareness in the trainer is not only valuable in assessing training effectiveness, but it also provides a watching brief on the trainer's own emotions, values, beliefs, assumptions and judgements.

It is often said by trainers that there are good courses and bad groups. Usually, the trainer is blind to a lack of skill on his part when he fails to achieve success, and consequently blames the group. The belief that learners are becoming less skilled in benefiting from training than they used to may imply a diminution in the *trainer's* skills – again a failure of awareness.

Effective trainers must be aware of their value judgements, and their possible effects on their training, in the range of potential disaster areas – attitudes in relation to equal opportunities, sex differences, prejudices developed from attitudes to race, colour, political and religious differences. It is not wrong for any trainer to have personal views and internal attitudes to any of these, but they must be very aware of these feelings and ensure that they are not letting them intrude on their training performance.

Sharing

The effective trainer is rarely one who works alone as a deliberate method of operation, although sometimes this is forced upon an individual. Awareness and development have been considered as desirable attributes for an effective trainer. These are virtually impossible in a closed situation. The aware trainers can assess the results of their behaviour, or think they can – these 'assessments' can be wildly inaccurate without feedback from others. Accumulation of knowledge can occur in isolation – reading books, watching films and videos, using computer programs, etc. But so much of our learning is from others, or in contact with others, when we can observe alternative approaches, sound out our ideas and innovations, and keep up to date on movements with which we might otherwise not be aware. Training is a 'people' job in so many ways, and the more contact with people the greater the likelihood there is of the trainer having a wider and more enlightened outlook.

Credibility

If the learners are to take any notice at all of the messages you are trying to convey, you must present a credible image. Different ways of achieving this are by:

- Being charismatic in spite of limited knowledge;
- Being charismatic in company with extensive knowledge;
- Being seen as an 'expert' or very experienced person in the subject;
- Having effective teaching skills;
- Having a behavioural pattern which does not offend the learners;
- Having a willingness to demonstrate that you can and want to learn yourself;
- Not projecting yourself as the 'expert';

and so on.

Visible timidity and uncertainty, tend to reduce credibility, particularly with some types and levels of learner, as does a demonstration of lack of knowledge of the subject. Credibility can also be reduced if the trainer behaves in an unacceptable way – criticizing in public members of the group, denying individual and group needs and rights, and failing to carry out promised actions. During one training course on which I was a student, the first three hours of the course were spent, at the invitation of the trainers, in determining our (the learners on the course) specific needs. After this activity, which raised our expectations considerably, our reported needs were simply ignored and the trainers proceeded with their pre-determined training programme. Both trainers and the training immediately lost any credibility in our eyes, to the extent that several of the learners left the event as soon as they saw what was happening.

Although the trainer holds initially a position of power over the group (whether sought or not), this can quickly dissipate if it is abused, with a loss of credibility.

Humour

In general, learning is more likely to be effective if the atmosphere in which it is conducted can be lightened at relevant times by some form of humour. This does not mean that the trainer must have an inexhaustible supply of jokes which can be used at any time, nor that the amount of learning equates with the amount of laughter emanating from the training room. An over-solemn approach can inhibit learning in many people, however, because the situation becomes too stressful. On the other hand, too light-hearted an environment can be unhelpful to learning, although it may be enjoyable.

A case in point is the attitude of different people to the different approaches in the videos available from various sources. Some of these feature well-known performers who create a great deal of laughter. Other productions approach the subject with less well-known, but equally capable actors using a more serious approach. Of course there are shades in-between.

Many people prefer the first type, saying that they learn because they take notice of the well-known performer and/or because the humour and laughter eases the situation and thus encourages learning. Many people take the opposite point of view in that they are distracted by the well-known cast who are seen as themselves, rather than the characters they are portraying, and the humour and laughter gets in the way of what, after all, is the 'serious' business of learning. This is one of the problems faced by the trainer when groups of 'mixed' learners are present at the event – and they are almost invariably mixed in a variety of ways. You certainly cannot satisfy all the learners all the time, so some form of compromise must be accepted.

To be effective, humour must be unforced and relevant, because forced humour is usually obvious and fails to be funny, and irrelevant humour can result in loss of credibility – 'Why on earth did he/she tell *that* story!!'. Humour must not be forced when the trainer is not a humorous person at all, although with practice and experience even this state can be improved. There are few things more capable of destroying a situation than a joke that fails.

Humour, however, need not be in the form of 'funnies'. In fact, the recounting of a relevant, humorous incident in which you were involved and preferably – which you were the victim, is often much funnier and seen as relevant humour. The effective trainer often builds up a bank of these anecdotes which can be introduced at relevant points and often relieve an over serious situation. Be careful of the 'supplied' anecdotes which may be used by several trainers – learners often attend training events by different trainers and if they hear the same anecdote recounted as a personal event by more than one trainer, they begin to be suspicious!

Therefore, in presentation skills humour is not an essential element, although it is often desirable at times and can give lighthearted relief if delivered in a natural and appropriate manner. Otherwise rely on knowledge, training skill and a friendly behaviour.

The effective trainer's sense of humour is not one which is directed outwards only. An effective trainer must have the ability to laugh at himself or lighten his emotions in some way, otherwise stress can build up to an unacceptable level. Every trainer has at some time had doubts about a number of things, had a 'bad' course, and thought 'that's it! I'm not putting myself through *that* any more'. It is often only resilience backed by a sense of humour which can pull someone out of this despondency – plus the knowledge that virtually every trainer goes through these emotions, not once in their careers, but usually many times.

Self-confidence

The final factor required in a trainer is confidence and the ability to transmit skills and knowledge to the learners. Many highly skilled and knowledgeable individuals are unable to act as trainers because they lack the confidence to stand up and impart their knowledge. The skills of presentation can be learned; the presentation content and method can be planned and prepared for; but even so a gap can exist which holds the individual back from having the self-confidence to stand up in front of what is, in the vast majority of cases, a friendly group of people.

Have you as a trainer, or have your trainers, these extra apparent qualities? I say, 'apparent' because the confident approach and appearance need only be superficial, at least in the early stages. The external image may be of confident, relatively nerveless skill, but underneath the presenter is a quivering mass of jelly! Which is the more important quality? It must the the *apparent* behaviour, because it is to the apparent image that the learners will be reacting. Like most performers who admit to having huge butterflies before going on stage, the trainer will experience nerves because the trainer is also a performer and the session a performance. The times when most trainers need to start worrying are when:

- They stop having stage fright symptoms, because this may mean they are no longer concerned about the level of performance they are about to give; or
- The butterflies stay with them, and may even increase throughout the session producing a less than effective performance.

If, however, this doesn't happen to you internally, do not worry that you are not a concerned trainer. Recently I heard a well-established actor say during a television interview that nerves did not affect him and he couldn't understand why it should 'because performing is my job and if I'm not capable of performing it, I shouldn't be doing it'. Perhaps, however, for most of us this is an extreme attitude.

Assessing the skills

The above descriptions detail seventeen specific skills which are required to a lesser or greater extent in every trainer, particularly those engaged in the wider or more elevated aspects of training and development. But the 90 per cent (at least) of us who cannot claim effectiveness in all or most of the skills must not give up hope. Learners excuse many aspects of a trainer's failings. Some degree of most of the skills must be present, to produce a reasonably effective trainer and absence of many must raise serious doubts about the person's ability to train effectively.

Most of the skills are observable and/or assessable, or at least the apparent behaviour related to the skills, and it is the observable behaviour which matters in most cases.

Skills alone do not make a trainer. Trainers of whatever nature are human beings and consequently vary from each other and the 'norm' to a considerable extent. In a meaningful assessment of trainers it is therefore necessary to have some measure of the rich variety that exists.

4

Trainer functions

The intrinsic behavioural skills of an individual are not the only measures which can be applied to the trainer. In the previous chapter we saw the various roles which might be demanded of a 'trainer' because of the type of training in which he is involved. Trainers are people, however, and as such reflect a wide variety of types and attitudes. From these attitudes and their related overt behaviours, trainers can be placed into categories, an understanding of which will help the assessor to understand more fully the person he is assessing.

The 'Townsend model'

At a reasonably 'tongue in cheek' level of assessment we find a three-dimensional model proposed by John Townsend (*JEIT*, Vol. 9, No. 3, 1985). He suggests that trainers operate, and hence take on type roles, in three dimensions:

1. Competence and/or knowledge in the subject matter being taught;
2. The skills of teaching the subject matter. These defined as:
    a) platform skills and other direct training skills
    b) the ability to put learning theory into practice
    c) the application of knowledge about adult learning
    d) the ability to design, prepare and organize material effectively;
3. Concern centred on the needs of the learners.

Figure 4.1 presents the typology as a three-dimensional matrix with the above components as the identifying features. Within each category there must be some grading, so that any category will have extreme,

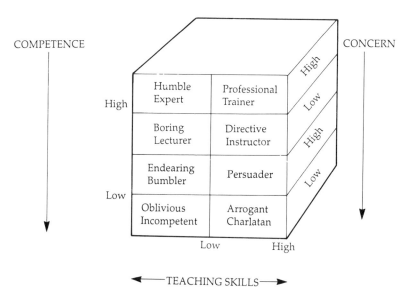

COMPETENCE   CONCERN

High

Low

Low   High

←——TEACHING SKILLS——→

Figure 4.1 The Townsend model
(Source: *JEIT*, Vol. 9, No. 3, 1985. MCB)

typical and weakly-represented members, in addition to a tendency towards a neighbouring, related type.

The Humble Expert

This category of trainer has *High Competence, Low Teaching skills and High Concern*.

The Humble Expert has an intimate knowledge of his subject is, as the name implies, a recognized expert. It would be very easy for him to present this knowledge in a way which would leave his audience in no doubt about his expertise. Because of the high concern for people and *their* learning requirements he is not likely to make that approach, but is more self-effacing and empathic. However, he does not have the teaching or training skills with which to capitalize on this approach, and consequently he is more likely to appear apologetic, being obtuse, disorganized and repetitive in the presentation of his material. His value is easily lost because of the lack of skills in presentation, unless the learners recognize the golden opportunity they have and work hard to extract the gold nuggets from this mine of information. It will require a very committed or sensitive group to take this action, a group that is intent on learning and does not mind what it does to achieve this. If a trainer type of this nature is recognized, amends can be made by attempting to instil in him training and teaching skills to back up the other desirable qualities. Sometimes it is the very expertise which is getting in the way and this difficulty must also be addressed.

The Boring Lecturer

In this case we have the category which has *High Competence, but both Low Teaching Skills and Low Concern.*

This is typical University or Polytechnic Lecturer who had dwelt in cloistered circles for many years, has produced a set of briefs which cover the material to be presented and uses these, almost unamended, for the rest of his career. Although this is a stereotype, examples do exist. And not only in the hallowed halls. Industrial and commercial training has its share of them. Usually they are to be found in environments where there is a high technical or technological input into the training, and they may be the highly qualified professional. In many cases, they are not full-time trainers, but are the guest speaker, introduced into an event because

1. They are the experts in the organization;
2. They are highly placed in the organization and 'like to support training';
3. They are used to fill an empty space in the training programme;
4. If the trainer had to take the subject session, he would have to prepare for it;

etc.

In many cases it is not the Boring Lecturer's fault that he falls into this category. Sometimes they are fully aware they are the experts, and in front of a group of learners they can't be bothered with the cosmetics of training and teaching techniques: those people are here to learn and here is the message from the expert's mouth. The developmental needs of an individual of this nature, who after all may be the trainer himself, are much greater than the Humble Expert. Training skills can be taught once the individual becomes (is made) aware of his shortcomings. There is also the question of attitude and concern for the learners. If the skills of training are accepted, relationship to the learners may be a spin off from this training. Awareness is not always as easily introduced as that, particularly in some of the more remote people who may not even accept that they are low in teaching skills, or, as indicated earlier, they feel they are not even necessary.

The Endearing Bumbler

Almost at the other end of the scale from our two experts who have little or no concern for people, this category is represented by *Low Competence, Low Teaching Skills, but High Concern* for people.

The endearing factor about this person is that, although they may approach their training tasks in a confused, disorganized, incompetent way, they are very concerned that they are dealing with people who are learners, and who are seeking help and guidance. Training events involving this type are likely to contain long lunch and refreshment breaks, may vary considerably from the programme because the trainer is *very* aware of the learners' needs (whether or not these relate to what should be taught) and reacts to these needs. Consequently, in spite of the bumbling, the delegates may learn something. However, this type of trainer, delightful though they may be as people, need to be taken in hand and introduced not only to teaching skills, but also to the need to prepare and have the relevant knowledge available. All this action must be taken without decreasing their concern for the people they have to train.

The Oblivious Incompetent

This all too common type is characterized by *Low Competence, Low Teaching Skills and a Low Concern* for people.

In some way they have entered the training field, have probably read a lot about knowledge and skills, without realizing what they meant, and in some way have reached the conclusion that they are highly skilled as trainers/teachers. Their false image of themselves blinds them to the fact that the learners are learning nothing from them – end-of-course validation sheets which give this message are brushed off as

Oh yes. That group was a very poor group.
'Happiness sheets' tell you nothing. I didn't set out to be popular. The end of course sheets are asking the wrong questions or the group has misunderstood what was being asked.
They just weren't bright enough to see the models, concepts, analogies I was presenting to them.

There are two basic ways to approach trainers of this type. They can be told of their failings by someone senior to them whom they recognize as being a skilled expert, and, if they accept the truths, can benefit from both skills and attitude training. Or, and it may be the more frequent solution, they can be transferred to where they do not have to be concerned about people and conveying information or skills, and where they can make direct use of whatever skills or expertise they might have.

The Arrogant Charlatan

Within this type is an interesting combination of *Low Competence, High Teaching Skills, and Low Concern* for people.

The principal motivation of this type of trainer is to present himself as a skilled trainer, slick in presentation and demonstration, giving the learners an exposition from which they should not be able to fail to learn. This attitude is based on the belief that you do not need to *know* the subject you are teaching, as long as you have learned all that is necessary for the session. The brief has been learned by heart, or is a detailed written document which is followed slavishly; the stage management notes are all carefully annotated – when to tell a joke, and which one; when to show a visual aid, etc. The visual aids are usually superb, because they have been copied from the original source – not necessarily with understanding – or have been prepared by someone else with real skill. The biggest problem this type of trainer has during a session is trying to fend off insistent questioning about material which is not covered by the brief. In this case the arrogance simply sweeps away, or ignores the questioning. Although the learners may initially be impressed by the apparent skill, the credibility gap soon becomes evident as the learners realize the limited extent of the knowledge and concern for their learning.

The remedies are again confrontation, followed by assistance with developing the people relationship factors and understanding the needs of the learners. The needs aspect will reflect the competence level which can be improved by a more realistic approach to preparation – the trainer should aim to have a wider knowledge than is necessary in the basic session brief. With a demanding learner group, knowledge is not the only essential; in addition there must be the knowledge/skill/adeptness to relate problems presented by the learners to the training and to real life. Consequently there must be a real *understanding* of what is being presented.

The Persuader

In this case the characteristics are those of *Low Competence, High Teaching Skills and High Concern*.

Many trainers fall into this category, particularly those corporate trainers who have to cover an extremely wide range of subjects. In such cases, the competence, i.e. knowledge and skills of a subject, may be relatively low, because they have to take on so many subjects, in many of which they will not have had first-hand working experience. Yet the organization requires them to train others in the subject. All they can do, particularly if time is short, is to learn as much as they can about the subject from books, experts, practitioners, etc. From this they will have to produce a satisfactory working brief, but with the awareness that the learners' demands may exceed this knowledge. The principal difference between the Persuader and the Charlatan is that the former has sufficient concern for the learners to admit openly this failing, but to take positive action to find out and report back whatever the learners want to know.

To succeed, the Persuader must have an extensive and relevant knowledge of training and learning techniques to ensure that the learners obtain as much as possible from their intervention. The Persuader uses these techniques as he wants to help the learners rather than because he wishes to demonstrate his/her own skill or give the learners only what he wants to give them.

In many ways the trainer who acts as a facilitator of learning, rather than operating in more of a teaching mode, is a Persuader who does not really need to have an in-depth knowledge of the procedures and methods within the subject. He is there to help the learners come to terms with the learning using their own resources. Obviously, so much the better if the facilitator also has the detailed competence, but at times this is either not possible or even necessary. The external provider of training is often in this situation.

The Directive Instructor

We have already encountered a role description of this type, but, if we look at inherent knowledge, skills and attitudes, the type has a *High Competence, High Teaching Skills, but a Low Concern for the learners*.

Much corporate training relates to the clerical, procedural, technical and technological skills required for the employees of the organization to be able to perform their tasks and duties. Fewer organizations look to the wider training needs of supervisors and managers at all levels in their less specific roles.

The Directive Instructor usually teaches on training courses using a set manual or training procedure, which rarely allows much in the way of variation in either content, structure or timing. If it is identified that the learners' needs differ in any way from the syllabus of the training event, little can be (is) done, not because the Instructor is not supportive to these needs, but because the course has to be run according to his directive. Often this is the correct way to go about the training – there is a set method, procedure of doing a job – and this must be taught so that this method and procedure is learned.

The unfortunate aspect of this type of trainer is that they have usually operated in the same way, for so long that when circumstances suggest that a different approach will be more effective they are unable to change. If the Instructor is in a training environment which demands instruction – well and good; if he is still an 'Instructor' in a rapidly changing environment which demands varied approaches, other than 'instruction', there can be many problems.

The Professional Trainer

Perhaps this is the ideal trainer type for all forms of training, except direct instruction described above. The characteristics of someone who fits this type are *High Competence, High Teaching Skills and High Concern* for people.

The word 'professional' here is used in its widest, supportive sense, rather than as a derogatory term. This type of trainer has a wide knowledge, experience, and above all understanding of a range of subjects; has detailed knowledge of a wide variety of training techniques, methods and applications *and* knows when to use each one to the most effective result; and has a strong concern for the learners. In his relationship with the learners, he can handle people in groups, large or small, face to face, in formal or informal situations, and is not averse to discussing, advising, even counselling out of training hours, perhaps in meal or refreshment breaks, or during 'bar' time.

There is always the danger that he will become too good, or be seen as such, but this should be less of a danger than in some of the other types, because of this skill and real concern for the learners.

How are these 'Super-Trainers' identified? Perhaps the principal evidence is in an absence of apparent stress in the trainer and a real absence of stress in the learners; an acceptance of the trainer in any situation by the learners (although he need not top the popularity polls); the readiness of the trainer to answer truthfully questions from the learners (and this includes the willingness to disclose a lack of knowledge – but a similar willingness to find out); a readiness to learn from the learners; a visible need to help the learners to learn and

45

transfer their learning to their real-life needs; and, above all, a positive and optimistic attitude to life and learning, practising what he preaches, thus demonstrating that the training messages do not originate in an unrealistic ivory tower.

Although Townsend's trainer type titles may appear lighthearted, they nevertheless represent the main types found amongst trainers, not necessarily because of the organizational role in which they have been cast, but because that is their preferred approach to training. Perhaps the real mark of the 'Professional Trainer' is his ability to be flexible and perform in some of the other roles as the occasion arises, without complaining that this is not the type of training he prefers.

The only category of Townsend's which I have altered is the 'Persuader'. Townsend called him the 'Shallow Persuader'. I felt that this was rather too harsh a name for what after all is the enforced and preferred role of many trainers – I know that I have been in this role more than once.

Learning styles

During the discussion about the trainer roles suggested by Townsend, referred to the trainer's typology being the result of their professional preferences – 'I want to be impressive'; 'I want to help these learners'; 'I must make sure that they learn the regulations,' etc. Trainers (people) may be considered in terms of their preferred approach. David Kolb in the United States pioneered the approach of categorizing people according to their preferred ways of learning, and this work has been continued in a modified way in Britain by Alan Mumford and Peter Honey in their 'Learning Styles'. Learning is part of life as a whole and I believe that the preferences shown for learning in the 'Learning Styles' is reflected in a much wider context of how we prefer (and often do) behave.

The preferences in the Honey and Mumford 'Learning Styles' are obtained by completing a questionnaire or inventory, which consists of 80 statements with which the completer has to agree or disagree whether the statement refers to them or not, by entering a tick or a cross. Typical statements are:

I have strong beliefs about what is right and wrong, good and bad.
I am attracted to more novel, unusual ideas than to practical ones.
I am careful not to jump to conclusions too quickly.
I am keen to reach answers via a logical approach.
I can often see better, more practical ways to get things done.

The responses are scored by totalling the number of ticks, i.e. the number of statements with which the learner agrees. Honey and Mumford have identified four main learning preference styles: Activists, Reflectors, Theorists and Pragmatists.

Activists are people who prefer to learn by doing something, even at times simply for the sake of doing it. They revel in innovative approaches, but having introduced the innovations tend to become bored with them and start looking for new fields. They are either the ones who jump in first when something has to be done or else they sit fuming internally thinking to themselves 'Why don't they just get on with it instead of rabbiting on!'. Watch the 'Activist' trainer when he has give the training group a task to perform, an inventory to complete, or asked them to sit and reflect on some aspect of the training. After the first minute it usually becomes obvious that he doesn't know what to do with himself while the others are working away! One can almost see him thinking: 'Why don't they get on with it?', 'Why are they taking so long?', 'Should I walk round the room or should I leave the room until they've finished?'.

Reflectors are interested in learning new concepts and practices but prefer to sit back and think about the implications, possible actions, etc. before saying or doing anything. They like to consider tasks and problems from all angles and are cautious before making a move. Often they are the very quiet members of the group and before they can come out with the results of their deliberations, the Activists have burst in and pressurized everybody into doing something – right or wrong. Reflectors can become very annoyed with the Activists who are interrupting their reflective processes, but the reverse does not necessarily apply. In fact the Activist is so busy 'doing' that he may not even notice the Reflectors reflecting!

Theorists are also in many respects reflectors, but their reflections are much deeper, and they insist on knowing, comparing and understanding the basic data, the assumptions, and the theories and models on which the ideas are based. They are the logical, rational and objective thinkers who like to take everything into consideration before reaching a decision. The basic criterion on which they work is 'If it can't be explained, I don't want to know'. Learning is limited if sufficient time is not given for them to consider, discuss, and argue the possibilities, and in doing so will certainly annoy the Activists and may even annoy the Reflectors who want some quiet to consider their own thoughts. It is quite common for people with a strong Theorist preference to have either an equally strong or moderately strong Reflector preference.

The *Pragmatists* are the practical people who are certainly interested in trying out new ideas, but only if it is shown that they have a practical, working value with specific and direct applications in the workplace. The subjective attitudes of the Activists are not for them. They are usually hard-working, fully involved people when a problem

47

has to be solved, or a task to be completed, but can disturb other preference types by their insistence on practical application.

It would be dangerous to attempt to apply a single label to individuals, particularly where the choice is only between four dominant types, but the 'Learning Styles' approach recognizes this and in practice people who complete the 'Learning Style' Questionnaire finish up with scores in all the four types. The distribution of these scores then becomes the important issue and application of the questionnaire to several thousand individuals has determined statistical distribution levels. From this distribution scores can be allocated within each style to preferences at very strong, strong, moderate and weak levels, where the boundary between the moderate and the strong levels determines the influence of that particular style. If the scores are above the 'norm', the style takes on a real meaning in that individual's preference approaches, although the extent of the scoring will also indicate the greater or lesser preference. For example, a score of about 11 or more in the Activist style will indicate that the individual has a strong preference for that style; below that score, this style does not become too much of an influence in that individual's life. The scores for Reflectors, Theorists and Pragmatists have a 'norm' with scores 14, 15 and 14 respectively. These are the norms for a wide, heterogeneous population of managers and supervisors. Specific norms are being constructed for particular groups such as Training Managers, Sales Managers, etc., although some groups have as yet insufficient examples to ensure that the profiles are valid.

Where individuals show a strong or very strong preference, there are a number of possible and usual permutations. People can have one style only as an 'above the line' preference – Activist, Reflector, Theorist or Pragmatist. Or there can be combinations of preferences – Reflector and Theorist, Reflector and Pragmatist, and Reflector-Theorist-Pragmatist. Perhaps the ideal is if all the styles are represented in an individual's profile at about the norm level or slightly above. This suggests that the individual is balanced and can utilize all the styles whenever the relevant occasion arises. Usually there is a bias towards one or two styles. Occasionally there are some strange bedfellows – the score indicates preferences in an individual for both Activist and Reflector. These in most respects are contrasting styles, and, if the questionnaire has been answered honestly and accurately, may suggest a conflict of interests and actions.

The four styles are linked directly with the four principal stages of the Learning Cycle in which total learning is achieved when something is done, experienced, actioned, etc. the experience is then considered in terms of what happened, when, how, by whom; questions are asked 'Was that the only way to do it?' 'What alternative approaches could have been taken?', 'How many alternative approaches are there?', 'Why did that happen/so and so do that?'. When everything has been taken into account and all the relevant information and learning extracted, plans can then be made about what should be done on the next occasion, in similar situations, and so on. The cycle is completed by further action, which is then reviewed, and so on.

If an individual has a strong preference for one style only, there is the danger that they can become locked in to one of the stages of the cycle and consequently not learn to the full extent.

Implications of the learning styles for trainers

If a trainer is locked in, albeit unconsciously, to a particular style, it is very likely that this attitude and preference will be reflected in the way he approaches his training function. The Activist is more likely to design events in which there is much happening, but may ignore the need to build in time for reflection. The Theorist trainer may become too involved in the intricacies of the 'hows' and the 'whys' and manipulate complex discussions which many of the learners may find uninteresting.

It may be, of course, that the organization using the trainer requires a particular style to be employed. If the trainer easily reflects this style, there is no problem, but if the required style is in conflict with the trainers' preferred styles, particularly if these are very strong preferences, difficulties may arise in the training. It is the responsibility of the trainer assessor to be aware of both the trainers' preferences and the organizational requirements, in addition to taking account of best training/learning practices.

A range of techniques is often called for, to balance the type of learning necessary with the learning needs *and* preferences of the learners. This level of training demands trainers with wide ranging preferences who are able to cope with changes in approach, without letting their personal dominant preference influence their work.

Conversely, in the 'Instructor' type of training, the very strong Activist who is unable to control his preference can be an embarrassment and can diminish the impact of the structured learning.

The assessor must also be aware that, although preferences are an intrinsic part of an individual, the strong preferences can be controlled by a determined individual allowing weaker preferences to develop. A subsequent benefit of the assessment might be help in an individual's development, once his preferences and their implications have been recognized.

Learning styles and trainer styles are closely allied, and the assessor must recognize that there are a number of factors at work in the determination of the trainer's role and function. Chapters 2, 3 and 4 have discussed some of the forces at work in forming these roles. The next chapter takes us forward with instruments designed to help in the identification of these various roles, functions and preferences.

5

Identifying trainer types

The Trainee-Content Training Inventory*

There are many different methods of considering the types and roles found amongst trainers and the ways in which they can meet the needs of the organization and the learner – our classical training trio. One of these, which has a direct relationship with both trainer attitudes and organizational attitudes, is known as the 'Trainee–Content Training Inventory' (T–C Inventory). This inventory compares the preferences, attitudes and activities of trainers in two dimensions. The first is 'Trainee Orientation' which is concerned with the trainer's attitudes and awareness, reflecting an emphasis on sharing authority and responsibility with the trainees versus an emphasis on retaining authority in the training situation. The other dimension is the 'Content Orientation' in which the trainer's choice is emphasis on the job of the trainer – the performance of task activities including planning and scheduling course content and evaluating trainee progress versus emphasis on role attributes – having the respect of trainees and colleagues, being an expert and evaluating trainee progress.

T–C Training Inventory background

Both of the orientations exist, of course, simultaneously in the behaviour of every trainer. A trainer can be highly trainee-orientated

*The inventory is reproduced with permission from Pfeiffer and Jones (Eds), the 1974 *Annual Handbook for Group Facilitators*, University Associates, 1974. It was originally entitled Student-Content Teaching Inventory.

and highly content-orientated at the same time. It is a trainer's personal philosophy that determines the emphasis he places on each orientation. Some trainers who feel that the needs of trainees and of the system are mutually exclusive and inevitably in conflict, strive to resolve the problem by concentrating on one or the other set of needs. Other trainers, while also feeling that a conflict between incompatible needs is inevitable, work toward some compromise or balance in which neither orientation is fully emphasized. Still other trainers see the trainee orientation and content orientation as functionally related. They aim to integrate trainee and system needs by emphasizing both.

In completing the Inventory the following should be kept in mind:

1. Many of the items are repeated. This is not to test the consistency of the participants' responses, as is the case in many instruments, but to relate the choices possible to a variety of circumstances.
2. Participants may find it difficult to choose the 'most important' statement of two equally attractive alternatives. The participant must choose one or the other.
3. Participants may find some items in which they feel both alternatives are unattractive. In such cases a choice must still be made, perhaps the 'least unattractive'.
4. Completion is best when tackled quickly – the immediate 'gut feeling' response – because too much consideration tends to increase the thoughts of 'Which is the best answer I should give?', rather than 'What do I really feel?'.

The Trainee–Content Training Inventory

The following questions concern your attitudes towards some training practices. Their purpose is to provide you with some indications for you to discuss about you as a trainer. There are no right or wrong answers: the best answer is the one most descriptive of your attitudes. Therefore, when answering the questions below, select the answer you feel to be true for you, as only realistic answers will provide you with useful information.

Each of the forty items consists of two statements, either about what a trainer can do or how they can behave. Circle the letter A or B in front of the statement you think is the more relevant to your feelings. In the case of some of the items you may think that both alternatives are important, but you should try to choose the statement you feel is *more* important. Sometimes you may think that both alternatives are unimportant: you should still choose the statement you think is *more* important.

It is more important for trainers to:
1. A. organize their courses around the need and skills of every type of trainee
   B. maintain definite standards of training performance

2. A. let the trainees have a say in course content and objectives
    B. set definite standards of training performance

3. A. emphasize completion of the course programme
    B. let trainees help set objectives and content

4. A. maintain trainees' progress by means of tests
    B. allow trainees a voice in setting course objectives and content

5. A. praise good trainees
    B. allow trainees to evaluate the performance of their trainers

6. A. allow trainees to make their own mistakes and learn from those experiences
    B. work to cover the course subject matter adequately

7. A. make it clear that they are the authority in the training situation
    B. allow trainees to make their own mistakes and to learn from their experiences

8. A. be available outside formal course hours to talk with trainees
    B. be available during course hours only

9. A. give tests to evaluate trainee progress
    B. tailor the course content to match the needs and abilities of each group

10. A. stay detached from the trainees
     B. let trainees plan their own programme according to their own interests

11. A. take an interest in the trainees as people
     B. make it clear that they are the authorities in the training situation

12. A. stay detached from the trainees
     B. be available outside formal course hours to talk with trainees

13. A. modify their position if one of the trainees shows where they were wrong
     B. maintain standards of performance

14. A. allow trainees to have a say in evaluating performance
     B. not socialize with the trainees outside course hours

15. A. see that the group covers the prescribed subject matter for the course
     B. be concerned about the trainees as people

16. A. let the trainees learn by experience
     B. maintain standards of training performance

17. A. allow trainees a voice in setting course objectives and content
     B. make it clear that they are the authorities in the training situation

18. A. discourage unnecessary talking during training sessions
     B. establish an informal atmosphere in the training situation

53

19. A. allow trainees to evaluate the training
     B. make it clear that the trainer is the authority in the training situation

20. A. stay detached from the trainees
     B. let the trainees make mistakes and learn by experience

21. A. be an authority on the course materials
     B. keep up to date in the field

22. A. be regarded as a person of high technical skills
     B. to update course materials constantly

23. A. to attend to his/her own personal development
     B. to be an authority on the course materials

24. A. to attend to his/her own personal development
     B. to set and example for the trainees

25. A. to ensure that each trainee is working to their full capacity
     B. to plan, in detail, all training activities

26. A. to construct fair and comprehensive validation methods
     B. to set an example for his trainees

27. A. to be known as an effective trainer
     B. to ensure that each trainee is working to his full capacity

28. A. to construct fair and comprehensive validation measures
     B. to ensure that the trainee is getting something from the course

29. A. to be an authority on the subject matter
     B. to plan and organize their course work carefully

30. A. to be a model for the trainees to emulate
     B. to try out new ideas and approaches on the course/group

31. A. to ensure that each trainee is working to their full capacity
     B. to plan and organize the course content carefully

32. A. to be available outside formal course hours to talk with trainees
     B. to be an expert on the course subject matter

33. A. to set an example for the trainees
     B. to try out new ideas and approaches on the group

34. A. to teach on a variety of courses
     B. to be a model for the trainees to emulate

35. A. to plan and organize training activities carefully
     B. to be concerned with the way the trainees are reacting

36. A. to be an authority on the course content
    B. to be known as an effective trainer

37. A. to give tests and evaluate trainee progress
    B. to be an authority on the course materials

38. A. to read journals relevant to the subject
    B. to be respected as a person of high technical skill

39. A. to be respected for knowledge of course subject matter
    B. to try out new ideas and approaches on the group

40. A. to be an authority on the course content
    B. to construct fair and comprehensive validation measures.

T–C Inventory Scoring
1. Draw a line under item 20
2. Items 1 to 20 comprise the T scale. Place an 'X' next to each item for which you have chosen the response indicated below.

Item	Response	Item	Response	Item	Response
1	A	8	A	15	B
2	A	9	B	16	A
3	B	10	B	17	A
4	B	11	A	18	B
5	B	12	B	19	A
6	A	13	A	20	B
7	B	14	A		

3. Items 21 to 40, which comprise the C scale are scored as above with the following 'answers

Item	Response	Item	Response	Item	Response
21	B	28	A	35	A
22	B	29	B	36	B
23	A	30	B	37	A
24	A	31	B	38	A
25	B	32	A	39	B
26	A	33	B	40	B
27	A	34	A		

4. The number of X's scored for items 1 to 20 are counted:
   The number of X's scored for items 21 to 40 are counted:
5. Next, both T and C scores should be plotted on the chart on the Summary Sheet. The score in the T box should be plotted on the left side (vertical scale) of the chart. The score in the C box should be plotted on the bottom (horizontal) scale of the chart. The participants make a mark where their T and C scores intersect.

T–C Inventory Scoring Chart
High
20

Strategy 2
Trainees do not really want to learn, but they will respond to trainers they like. The trainer's primary responsibility is to win trainees over so they can be taught.

Strategy 5
Trainees like all people learn and explore. A trainer's primary responsibility is to integrate trainee and system needs by creating a learning climate and making learning meaningful and relevant.

15

Strategy 4
Trainee and system needs are incompatible. It is of primary importance that something be taught, but trainee needs cannot be ignored. The trainer's first responsibility is to push them enough to get the work done but also to do something for them to maintain training session morale.

10

T 5

Strategy 3
Trainees are lazy and indifferent to learning. Since a trainer is helpless to change the situation his primary responsibility is to present the information the system requires.

Strategy 1
Trainees do not want to learn, but they will respond to strong direction and control. A trainer's primary responsibility is to make sure the material gets taught.

0   5   10   15   20
Low   Content Orientation   High

The T–C Training Inventory: the five training strategies

Five 'pure' training strategies (or styles) result from a) the interaction of the trainee and content orientations and b) the differing degrees of emphasis which trainers place on each orientation. The five styles are discussed below and depicted on the scoring graph.

Strategy 1

The strategy at the lower right corner of the diagram defines the style of a trainer whose basic philosophy dictates that trainee and system needs are mutually exclusive. Thus, this trainer resolves the conflict by placing maximum emphasis on content orientation and minimum emphasis on trainee orientation.

For this trainer the syllabus defines what should be (or perhaps what the organization has decreed). Since trainees may resist training and learning, the trainer's primary responsibility is to ensure that material *is taught*. It is important to set definite standards of training performance and to check continually to see that trainees are meeting the standards sought. This is accomplished by giving frequent spot tests, attending all training sessions, etc.

Strategy 2

This trainer, whose strategy appears at the upper left corner of the diagram, also feels that trainee and system are incompatible and in conflict. Like his Strategy 1 colleague, this trainers feels that trainees really do resist training and learning, but he disagrees that the basic conflict can be overcome by tight training session control. Instead this trainer places maximum emphasis on trainee orientation, minimum emphasis on content orientation.

Trainees will learn from trainers they like – so being liked is both necessary and personally gratifying for this trainer. They feel that a trainer's primary responsibility is to be supportive and to win the 'friendship' of their trainees. This is accomplished by putting on a 'good show' in the training session, ignoring attendance, allowing trainees to set their own course standards, socializing etc.

Strategy 3

Like his Strategy 1 and 2 colleagues the trainer whose strategy is defined in the lower left corner of the diagram also believes in the conflict of trainee and system needs, and in trainees' resistance to learning. Unlike his colleagues he feels helpless to deal with the situation. Trainees will learn what they want to learn, when they want to learn it. A trainer simply cannot change this fact. Thus, the trainer's primary responsibility is to present the information and follow his job description. If the trainer has a 'good' group of trainees, he is lucky: if he has a 'bad' group, there is nothing he can do about it. Those trainees with initiative and motivation will learn. For Strategy 3 trainers, their philosophy justifies mechanistic presentations. At the higher training level these trainers may prefer to teach 'advanced seminars' and shun the basic core courses.

Strategy 4

At the middle of the diagram is the strategy of other trainers who believe in the basic incompatibility of trainee and system needs. They aim instead for a compromise, or balance, by fully emphasizing neither the trainee orientation nor the content orientation.

Both system-needs and trainee-needs matter, but these trainers cannot see how to put them together. They end up with a moderate level of concern for each. Thus, the system requires the trainers to give forms of testing, but they may specify the exact resources from which questions/tasks will be drawn, rather than using those decreed by the system.

Strategy 5

At the upper right corner of the diagram is the strategy of the trainer who believes that trainees are always learning. In the mind of this trainer, the trainee and the system needs are not inevitably in conflict.

The aim is to *integrate* both sets of needs by placing maximum emphasis on both trainee and content orientations.

These trainers feel that a trainer's primary responsibility is not to see that something is *taught*, but rather that something is *learned*. Thus it is important to create a climate in which learning is meaningful and relevant. Learning activities are structured to bring maximum benefit to the trainee, the training system and the trainer.

The preceding descriptions are clearly caricatures of trainer behaviour: they are not intended to be descriptions of real people. Certainly there are as many different training strategies as there are trainers. The strategy descriptions exaggerate behaviours that differentiate types of trainers, not to simplify behaviour, but to make it more understandable. If the strategies are defined and people are aware of them, they can be changed.

The T–C Training Inventory is one way of opening this process by providing a vocabulary, a model and experiences on which to focus one's own behaviour.

Trainer role orientation

The T–C Training Inventory is but one of the many instruments available to help trainers analyse their attitudes and preferences towards training. It would be simple to reproduce many of these, but that might not be helpful here. Other than the 'Learning Styles' analysis of Honey and Mumford and the T–C Inventory, I recommend the use of a third valuable instrument, the Trainer Orientation Framework constructed by Andrew Pettigrew.

Four predominant trainer types are identified by using this framework, based on their attitudes and orientations to work, and within this, two polarized factors are emphasized. The first relates to the orientation of the trainer with respect to the way they present their material and relate to the learners. At one extreme the trainer sees training as very similar to the traditional educational process in which courses are set up, based on the requirement to achieve set training objectives. Subject matter is researched thoroughly and developed for a formal and structured presentation to the learners. The course is well timetabled and is seen as a mechanism for the transfer of knowledge, skills and attitudes from the 'expert' trainer to the learners. A very trainer-centred approach is developed which requires complete fulfilment of the training objectives determined before the programme.

Alternatively, the trainer takes a much more flexible attitude and considers that he has the responsibility to determine the organizational needs, and produce a range of interventions in the training programme which will satisfy them. Trainers in this mode will not be confined or contained in any way by the traditional approaches, rather they will be innovative and experimental, and very sensitive to the needs and emotions of the learners. Programmes approached in this style are very learner-centred.

The other factors are concerned with the organization within which the training is performed. At one extreme the trainer sees the training as maintaining the smooth running of the organization. Existing systems, procedures, technologies and methods are there to be instilled in the learners because this is the corporate need. Problems and needs are addressed in a 'fire-fighting' approach, as they arise.

At the other extreme, change is the paramount feature of the trainer's attitude. He sees training as the mechanism of change, changing the systems, procedures, technologies and methods in an effort to make improvements. To this trainer type, training is not the only trainer function, but organizational needs and change must be assessed and anticipated, and the trainer is a principal agent in preparing other people for change.

The trainer's attitudes to these factors can be assessed or self-assessed and a role orientation identified. The general descriptions above relate to the extremes: positions will be taken on all points of the continuum.

Trainer orientation questionnaire

The questionnaire approach suggested to identify the trainer orientation in this model is a much simpler one than that in the preceding inventory and other similar models. However, this simplicity is deceptive, for the user must think carefully about his attitudes, preferences and practices before being able to answer the two questions. I am indebted to the Manpower Services Commission (now the Training, Enterprise and Education Division of the Department of Employment) and the Institute of Training and Development for this questionnaire which appears in *Guide to Trainer Effectiveness*, MSC/ITD, 1984.

1. Do you have an orientation to the maintenance needs of your organization, that is, to ensuring the continuance of the existing activities, products or services? Or do you have an orientation to bringing about change within the organization, that is, to ensure that training can respond to pressures for change from both outside and inside the organization to help it get geared up to meet new situations, objectives, etc. Mark on the scale below where you think you are.

    Maintenance   Change
    orientation   orientation
    ....
           0   1   2   3   4   5   6   7   8   9   10

2. Do you have an orientation to traditional methods of training, that is, methods

and approaches based on the educational or 'professional' model of training, based largely on classroom-based techniques and curriculum design? Or do you have an orientation to methods of intervention, that is, a 'change agent' approach to training that involves greater participation in bringing about changes in systems, procedures or technologies and in changing peoples' attitudes and approaches to work? Mark on the scale where you think you are.

Traditional educational orientation

Interventionist orientation

0   1   2   3   4   5   6   7   8   9   10

3. Now transfer the scoring information from (1) and (2) to the framework in figure 5.1. Mark the place where both points coincide.

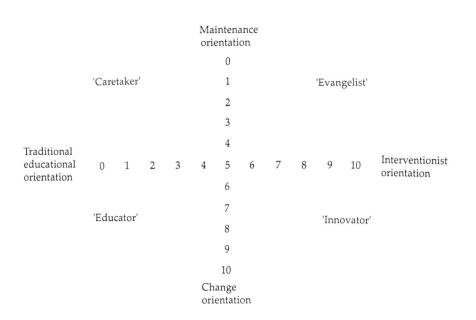

Figure 5.1 Role orientation
(Source: *Guide to Trainer Effectiveness*. MSC/ITD, 1984)

Where the point is located on the framework indicates the preferred trainer role orientation, but it must be remembered that the emphasis of that role will depend on the position within the quadrant, suggesting a typical, extreme or 'weak' member of that role, and a close or distant relationship with other role(s).

Role orientation: the four predominant types

Type 1: 'Caretakers'
Caretakers see the need for training to maintain the smooth running of present systems, procedures and technologies in the organization and adopt traditional educational approaches. They typically use trainer-centred training approaches, structure programmes highly and respond to training needs as presented to them by someone in authority.

Type 2 'Educators'
Unlike the 'caretaker', the 'educators' see the need for training to change systems, procedures and technologies in the organization, but like the 'caretakers' tend to adopt traditional educational approaches. They anticipate the need for change and work strategically by setting training objectives and designing and timetabling appropriate training programmes.

Type 3 'Evangelists'
Evangelists see the need for training to maintain present systems, procedures and technologies in the organization, but adopt a range of interventionist approaches. Basically, they feel that traditional educational approaches are inappropriate and attempt to convert people in the organization to accepting a range of learner-centred experiences in the form of, say, workshops, seminars and consultancy. They see their role more as a facilitator of learning than an expert on the subject matter.

Type 4 'Innovators'
Innovators see the need for training to change systems, procedures and technologies in the organization and adopt a range of interventionist approaches. They are particularly pervasive in the organization in order to understand the real needs that exist. They persuade people to become involved and guide them through a problem-solving process rather than proposing solutions. In essence they are catalysts or change-agents.

Trainer type inventories: their uses

All the inventories and questionnaires described so far are principally for self-assessment, and as such are invaluable for the trainer in a process of assessing his or her own preferences and attitudes. However, their use can be much wider than this in the general area of trainer effectiveness assessment. The training manager who is the principal interested party, other than the trainers themselves, in assessing effectiveness can also use the inventories in a variety of ways.

Before an assessor can assess someone else, it is useful for that assessor to have a good knowledge of his or her own attitudes, preferences and beliefs. This knowledge will help the assessor to recognize bias against the person he is assessing due to differences between them. For example a training manager whose background has been very much in the 'instructor'/'theorist'/'educator' roles and orientations may have difficulties in assessing a trainer whose roles and orientations are much more towards the 'Persuader'/'Activist'/'Innovator'. If the assessor is aware of these differences, and can identify the activities which relate to them, there is a much better likelihood of a fair assessment being made, in spite of the two people being at almost completely opposite ends of the attitude spectrum.

A complete knowledge, understanding and awareness of the results of inventories and models such as these will help the assessor in these realistic assessments. Attitudes and preferences in themselves are insufficient for organizational and corporate assessment purposes however. A trainer's effectiveness within an organization may depend on whether he or she meets *the demands of the organization*. There is little point in a trainer adopting the 'innovator' role when the learning needs and the organizational culture demand an 'instructor' approach. The trainer orientation and the organization needs must be congruent. If they are not, and this becomes evident in the assessments, several options are available.

- The trainer can accept that the needs of the organization are different from his own orientation, so he can and will adapt to the organizational requirements.
- The trainer can accept that the needs of the organization are different from his own orientation, so he can and will adapt to the organizational requirements, but will steadily attempt to introduce changes which can be made acceptable to the organization and come nearer to his orientation.
- The trainer can accept that the differences exist, but realizes that the two requirements are not only incongruent but he cannot compromise his beliefs. Consequently the only action is to terminate that employment and seek an organization which has a compatible culture.

There are of course alternative strategies, but all require compatibility between the trainers' current actions and the needs of the organization. It is this compatibility that is what the assessor is assessing, whether we are considering self-assessment or manager-assessment.

6

The uses of training validation

The skills of the trainer and the content of the training are inextricably intertwined. Both a training manager who has a number of trainers and observes them in action over a period of time and a learner who attends various courses with different trainers are aware of a mixture of effects. A good trainer with good material will produce a highly effective course; the same trainer with poor material will produce a poorer course, although not totally ineffective because his skill and experience will help to redeem the material. A poor trainer given good material will produce an ineffective learning experience however, salvaged only perhaps by skilled learners who want to learn and do so in spite of the trainer; a poor trainer with poor training material gives the learners no chance at all.

From this it is clear that in addition to any assessment of the trainer's skills, a review must be undertaken of the training material, its completeness, currency, necessity and effectiveness. In many cases, this assessment must be subjective because of the nature of the training; in others, objective tests and examinations can be applied.

Every occupation and industry has its own jargon to describe its terms and processes. In training the words 'validation' and 'evaluation' and even 'assessment' are commonly used, although this is complicated by the conflict in their use by people not only in different professions, but also within the same profession!

General dictionaries do not help much, being vague in their definitions. To validate is to 'make valid (sound, defensible, well-grounded), ratify, confirm'. To evaluate is to 'ascertain amount of, find numerical expression for, appraise, assess' and even 'determine the value of'. Assessment is 'the act of assessment, fixing the value of, a valuation' (usually applied in general dictionaries to a form of monetary valuation).

Within the professions interested in these subjects, there is little consistency. Some psychologists and trainers use the three words in a completely interchangeable way; others use one of them to mean all three effects; others have specific definitions which are in direct conflict with the definitions of others!

Some years ago, the British Manpower Services Commission attempted to produce a standardized glossary of training terms to help the language of training. My own approach is to accept these definitions as effective working definitions.

The MSC definitions for 'validation' are:

1. Internal validation. A series of tests and assessments designed to ascertain whether a training programme has achieved the behavioural objectives specified.
2. External validation. A series of tests and assessments designed to ascertain whether the behavioural objectives of an internally valid training programme were realistically based on an accurate initial identification of training needs in relation to the criteria of effectiveness adopted by the organization.

Whether or not these definitions appear too complex and wordy, if they are examined closely they serve not only as a definition, but also set out the training application actions necessary before validation can be approached – 'behavioural', 'objectives', 'realistically based', 'initial identification of training needs', 'criteria . . . organization'. Without the application of these activities, any subsequent validation ceases to have any value.

The definition of 'evaluation' is:

The assessment of the total value of a training system, training courses or programme in social as well as financial terms. Evaluation differs from validation in that it attempts to measure the overall cost benefit of the course or programme and not just the achievement of its laid down objectives. The term is also used in the general judgemental sense of the continuous monitoring of a programme or of the training function as a whole.

Finally, the MSC defines 'assessment' as:

A general term for the process of ascertaining whether training is efficient or effective in achieving prescribed objectives. It covers both validation and evaluation.

My simpler explanation of these definitions is that 'evaluation' covers training and its real benefits at work from beginning to end, whereas validation concentrates on the effectiveness of the training itself in relation to the training alone. 'Assessment' is the process of measuring both validation and evaluation.

What we want to know

Whatever words we use to describe what we are doing or what we should be doing and achieving, the aim is to ensure that our training is effective for both the learner and the organization. This means that we need to ask certain questions and obtain meaningful answers; these questions will include both 'validation' and 'evaluation' as defined earlier:

1. Has the training satisfied its objectives?
2. Has the training satisfied the objectives/the learning needs of the clients?
3. Can it be demonstrated at the end of the training that these objectives have been met?
4. Are people operating differently at the end of, and as the result of, the training?
5. Did the training contribute directly to this different behaviour?
6. Could the behavioural change have been obtained in a different way?
7. Is the learning achieved being used in the real work situation?
8. Has the training/learning contributed to the production of a more efficient and effective worker?
9. Has the training contributed to a more effective and efficient (hence more cost and value-effective) organization?

Validation questions
More specific questions are raised in order that we might validate and evaluate the training provided.

Training content
Is the material contained in the training programme complete to the extent of the required criteria? Is it relevant to the skills, knowledge or attitudes being presented? Is it up to date? Are there processes established to maintain these requirements?

Training methods
Are the methods, techniques and approaches the most appropriate ones for this subject, this level and status of learner, etc.? Were the methods used the most appropriate for the learning styles of the learners?

Learning amount
What was the material included in the course? Was it new to the learner or, perhaps because prior knowledge had not been determined, repeated, known material? In spite of being repeated material, did this repetition materially assist the learners to come to terms more effectively with the material?

Length and pace of the training
If the material included satisfied the content criteria, was the event of an effective length and pace? Were all aspects afforded their required time and emphasis? Were some areas laboured and others skimped?

Objectives
Did the training event satisfy its stated behavioural objectives? Were the learners given any opportunity to try to satisfy their personal objectives? Was this opportunity accepted? Were personal objectives actually satisfied?

Omissions
Were any essential aspects omitted from the learning event? Did time constraints, excess material, incorrect approaches contribute to these omissions?

Transfer to work
How much of the learning is likely to be transferred to work on the learner's return there? What are the factors which will encourage or inhibit this transfer? To what extent will the learner's manager be involved in this transfer?

Relevance
Was the course/seminar/workshop/conference/tutorial/coaching assignment/project/open learning system, etc. the most appropriate means of approaching these learning needs? Would more or as much learning have been achieved by some other application? Would as much learning have been achieved without any training intervention?

Environment
Was the training environment the most appropriate for the learning – hotel, conference centre, organization training establishment, space at the work establishment (training room, rest room, etc.), at the person's

workplace? Were the environmental conditions conducive to learning – comfort, heating, noise, visibility, etc.? Were the domestic arrangements satisfactory – food, sleeping accommodation, study accommodation, etc.?

Finally, and very relevant to the overall subject of this book

The trainer
Did the trainer have the necessary skills, knowledge, attitudes, techniques, approaches and methods to present the material in such a way that learning was encouraged?

Evaluation questions

Questions will need to be asked following the validated training events to ensure that the training/learning is in fact put into operation for the benefit of the learner and the organization. Examples of questions of evaluation are:

Application of learning
Which elements of the individual's work now include elements which are a direct result of the training event? Which new aspects have already been introduced as a result of the learning? Which parts of the previous work have now been replaced or modified as a result of the training and learning? Which relevant and accepted elements of the training have not yet been applied? Why not?

Efficiency and effectiveness
How much more efficient and/or effective is the level of work now being achieved? Is this the result of the training? If not, how has it been achieved?

Training hindsight
With the passage of time and attempts to apply the learning, are there any amendments to the end-of-training validation responses which were given?

The questions relating to the validation of the training will normally be posed either at the end of the training programme or soon after its conclusion, the evaluation questions at a later stage. At this later stage, some 3, 6 or 12 months following the end of the training, the questions can be asked of both the learner and the learner's manager, both of whom should state their own particular viewpoints. As we discussed earlier, the line manager must be interested in this process for the training to have any effectiveness.

The validation trail

Validation should not be confined to the end of the training event, although it is only too common for the trainer, training manager or senior management to ask for validation:

- Immediately after the start of the training course;
- During the progress of the training course;
- At the end of the training event;
- Some time after the actual end of the event.

Under such circumstances validation has no value whatsoever. The basic requirement of any form of validation or evaluation is to have some measure of the learner's starting point before the training. If the learner's level of knowledge, skill or attitude is not known before the training starts, it will be impossible to assess whether there has been any improvement. Improvement over what? Often, at the end of a training event, it is said: 'Oh yes. They have all improved considerably'. This is a statement with no value whatsoever.

Before we can start looking at any measures for validating the training event, it is necessary to consider what can and must be done prior to the training.

Training analyses

The training trail will begin in some way with a training needs identification. Needs are often expressed without any real analytical approach: 'It would be a good thing if such and such a training course was put on'! I am assuming here that someone in an organization has determined that training in certain aspects is necessary for the well-being of the organization individuals and the organization itself. An analysis of this nature will have been obtained from such events as:

- The introduction of new work;
- The injection into the organization of a number of inexperienced workers;
- Direct observation that certain aspects of work are not being performed effectively;
- Indirect evidence (for example, a reducing number of sales or

production of items or continuance of clients) that certain areas of the work are not being performed effectively;

- A request by individuals or groups of individuals for training in certain subjects for whatever reason;
- The completion of annual job appraisal reports which show some training need;
- The introduction of a development programme;

and so on.

Many of these pieces of 'evidence' that training is required will be simply little more than an indication and it will be necessary for a more detailed analysis to be performed. This book is not the place for a full description of these essential activities, but the next requirement is usually for the production of a very specific job description or specification linked with a person specification. The matching or non-matching of these two factors will determine the skill gaps and hence the training specification.

This approach will be particularly relevant in the analysis situations shown above where:

- New work is being introduced;
- Inexperienced workers are being recruited;
- Work is not being performed effectively;
- Development is seen as necessary.

Job analysis, description and specification

The job description

The job description is the first level of the final job specification or task analysis, which describes the job, at the responsibility level, in a fairly general way. In some analyses these are known as Key Purposes, or Units of Work, or, in Management by Objectives approaches, as Key Result Areas or Tasks. Within a job description are given the principal areas of work and responsibility, and such aspects of the job as lines of responsibility and communication, hours of work, etc. A typical job description for a hotel receptionist is shown in Figure 6.1.

Job Title:	Hotel Receptionist
Function:	To maintain the hotel's bookings, reservations and charge system, and be the hotel's principal customer contact point.
Lines of Communication	Upwards – to Head Receptionist Laterally – to other Receptionists Downwards – to Junior Receptionists and Hall staff
Responsibilities	To – Head Receptionist For – Junior Receptionists

Hours of work	Shift system (detailed according to practice)
Duties:	1. Dealing with room reservations made by telephone, letter, Telex and customer contact.
	2. Allocating reservations and completing records of these reservations.
	3. Confirming reservations with customers by the appropriate means.

Figure 6.1 Example of a job description

The job description is too broadly described to be useful in identifying training needs and presents only the baseline for the full description of a job, its duty requirements and responsibilities. It does supply an outline and starting point from which more detailed requirements can be identified.

The job specification

The job specification enlarges upon the job description and it is here that the areas where possible training needs are found. In the specification each general area of responsibility or unit of work is examined carefully to produce a detailed requirement of the job. The specification offers in detail what the job holder *should* be able to know and do, and identifies the attitudes and manner needed to perform the job effectively.

An example of a straightforward job specification, or at least part of it, is shown in Figure 6.2. A painter and decorator has a number of units of work, one of which is paperhanging. Part of the job specification for the paperhanging element of the painter and decorator's work is shown.

Job Title:	Painter and Decorator.
Duties:	3. Paperhanging
	3.1 Task: Selection of paper
	Knowledge: Types of wallcovering, including the strengths, textures etc. of the materials
	Skills: Ability to assess covering quantity by manual manipulation.
	3.2 Task: Measuring room
	Knowledge: Methods of estimation, unit methods of measurement
	Skills: Measuring in various unit methods etc.

Figure 6.2 Example of part of a job specification

In this example, only some of the elements of one unit of work have been given, divided into knowledge, skills and attitudes. There will be other elements concerned with the preparation for paperhanging, the actual paperhanging, and the post-task operations.

The more detailed and complete the job specification, or task analysis, the more likely it is that the training needs analysis will be sufficiently accurate and comprehensive. This analysis is the first line of attack in producing terminal training objectives for the training event, the measures by which the effectiveness of the training can be assessed.

Training objectives

The difference or 'gap' between the identified, detailed needs of the job in terms of knowledge, skills and attitudes, and the knowledge, skills and attitudes of the job holder or potential job holder determine the training needs, the so-called training gap. Once it has been decided that training should be given to fill this gap, the trainers can start designing a training event to satisfy these needs. The *end* of the training – the terminal training objectives should be considered first. These objectives will describe in as much active detail as possible, what, at the end of the training event, the learners will know, be able to do, and what their attitudinal behaviours will be – the training needs from the Job and Person Specification described as end results. If, at the end of the training, the learners with these particular needs can show that they have satisfied the training objectives and hence have satisfied their training needs, the training can be assessed as successful.

The training event can then be designed with these objectives in mind, taking account of all the factors we have already considered to ensure that the learning is achieved in the most effective way.

The next step, in association with pre-training measures, is to design the end-of-training validation instruments. An important part of that statement, and one which is often ignored, relates to the 'pre-training' measures. Again we return to the truism 'If you don't know where you have come from, how will you know how far you have come and whether the end of the journey has been achieved?'.

Pre-training assessment

In most cases, training events have been designed for groups of individuals with common learning needs. Within these groups, virtually every individual has a different need, and different levels of knowledge, skills and attitude. It would be too much to expect that each learner would have exactly, or even be close to, the same level of need! Consequently it is necessary for the training to be designed, not only to satisfy the overall terminal objectives, but also to cope with the individual needs. Some form of pre-training assessment is clearly required – we shall look at ways of doing this in the following chapter.

It was also suggested earlier that the learning might have been achieved without the individuals attending a training course or receiving some other form of instruction. Some form of comparison is necessary to ensure that any learning is as a result of training. To do this we can use control groups.

A control group is a group of people with attributes as similar as possible to the group being trained. As an ideal they would be identical in organization employment, job, age, sex, experience, education, intelligence and skill level, although the complete match of this nature is very unlikely (if not impossible) in practice. An attempt must be made to achieve this ideal as nearly as possible.

If possible, more than one control group should be used to reduce to a minimum any selectivity errors. In practice, it is extremely difficult to obtain one control group; more than one is almost impossible in normal working situations.

Unlike the training group, the control group receives no training, but in order to produce a parallel assessment, they undertake any pre- and post-training validation and interviews in which the training group is involved.

When all the assessment measures have been undertaken with both the control and the training groups, analyses are undertaken to assess what learning changes have taken place. The validation measures should show that there has been a positive change in the learning group. If the control group shows a similar change over the same period, and it can be shown that there are no special circumstances to explain this change, the value of the training is suspect. If the control group shows some measures of change, the extent of these changes should indicate to the trainer that there should be a re-examination of the training course to eliminate unnecessary material. If the control group shows no change at all, this gives support to the validity and value of the training, and suggests that the changes in the training group have been due to the training.

Training design

Once the job specification has been firmly established and the training needs of the population identified as accurately as possible, the training staff can proceed with the design of an appropriate training programme. This should reflect:

- The training needs identified from the task and person analyses broken down into manageable learning blocks;
- The training content relevant to the needs of the individual and the organization;

- The course/workshop/seminar/sessions/learning package pitched at the appropriate level;
- The specific terminal objectives which are, as far as possible, quantifiable, active, measurable and time bounded;
- The learning preferences of the learners taken into account as far as they are known and as far as the training will allow;
- Learner involvement to the optimum extent;
- The insertions of appropriate tests/validations at the relevant times;
- Selection of the most appropriate and effective trainers for the event;
- Selection of the most appropriate environment available for the event.

These requirements should be met by whoever is to be responsible for the training validation (and subsequently the trainer assessment) for an assessment of the competence level of the training and its design. The planning and design factors, as we saw earlier, are highly indicative of the skills of an effective trainer, and as such will feature strongly in any assessment of the training and the trainer.

It will be difficult for any potential assessor, other than in self-assessment, to have direct access to the planning and design activities of the trainer and consequently to have a full knowledge of all the elements which have led to the design of the training. The effective trainer should have satisfactory documentation to show and support the steps taken, in job and task analysis, needs analysis and plans for implementation leading to the training design, the plans for the presentation of the training (including notes on techniques, methods, approaches, activities, etc.), and details of the validation actions. Without these, the assessor – whether the training manager or the trainers themselves – cannot ensure valid assessment of the training.

7

Training validation at work

In the previous chapter the value of assessing the training event as part of the assessment of the trainer was considered. Perhaps this area of assessment in training has distracted attention from measures to assess the trainer. Although approaches to training validation are many and varied, it is surprising how many organizations involved in training give little priority, if any, to training validation.

In any consideration of the effectiveness of a trainer or group of trainers the effectiveness of the training itself must be a powerful measure in addition to direct assessment of the trainers themselves. Training validation is one of the more objective measures that the trainers can utilize if they are embarking on self-assessment. Some assessors assert that the training validation is all that is necessary, because if the measures show that the training is valid, the trainers themselves must be effective. This is a strong argument, but requires much supportive evidence. If a particular training event is an infrequent one and the validation measures of one course show its effectiveness, this demonstrates effectiveness for that course and with that trainer on that occasion only. The next similar course, with or without the same trainer, may be a disaster.

Assessment of the trainer will also give additional information about whether there are any particular strengths or weaknesses which can be improved or utilized more effectively in other situations. Although the course validations show effectiveness, this may or may not be due to the trainer – there are intelligent trainees! – and if the trainer, who may not be completely effective, is helped to improve, the training may become even better, and certainly in some cases more pleasurable and an easier learning event for the trainees.

These are but a few of the reasons why both approaches are necessary. Assessment can be made using either, but there are benefits in using both.

Training inventories

Assessment instruments are required for assessing knowledge, skills and/or attitudes at various stages of training. There will be, of course, some aspects of training which are not sufficiently sensitive to measurement to permit completely objective assessment. Many of these are the human relations type of training. Such training areas as people skills, interpersonal and interactive 'skills' and even the more apparently objective types of people training such as leadership, supervision, presentation, etc. have varying degrees of objectivity and consequently affect the assessment. Some assessors even suggest that some forms of training, for example management training, cannot be measured by validation. I cannot agree, although I accept that there are aspects of training which are highly subjective, in which case it is necessary to use more subjective forms of assessment, accepting their subjectivity and making allowances. Is it not better to attempt something, than to do nothing at all, however imperfect that something might be?

The assessment of the effectiveness of such training as interpersonal skills is particularly difficult. Assessment might be made by an external observer – what are the standards of interpersonal effectiveness to which *that individual* works? Are they the same as others'? Are they in line with an 'accepted' model? etc. Can an individual assess his/her own relationships effectiveness, as we so often ask them to do? Again, what standards are they using in this self-assessment?

Assessments can be made, even in these difficult areas. For example, the external observer may use Behaviour Analysis, an accurate form of behaviour observation and recording, but one which requires a subjective model of behaviour from which to work. If self-assessment is required, the classical pre- and post-tests fall down for a variety of reasons. Modification of this, such as the Three-test, can be introduced which reduces *some* of the inherent subjectivity.

When technical, procedural, systems, etc. types of training are considered, assessment of the effectiveness of the training is relatively simple. For example, the objective of a training course for newly appointed gas meter readers might be expressed as 'By the end of the training each person will be able to read 100 meters of the clock variety to an accuracy of 95% during a period of "x" minutes'. Two tests would be necessary for this training. Before the training started, it would be necessary to set a practical test of meter-reading for the trainees – for example, 100 meters might be made available and the trainees given the instruction to read as many of them in 'x' minutes as possible. The number of meters read during the period and the reading accuracy could then be measured. At the end of the training the same test would be repeated (the classical pre- and post-test procedure) and if the objective stated above was fulfilled by all the trainees, the training would obviously have been 100% effective. If this situation was repeated with a number of different instructors and the same results achieved, there would be every indication that the training content, methods, etc. were the contributory factors to the success rather than the trainers.

Not all training is as straightforward as this, however, and when we come to the assessment of the more subjective training subjects mentioned earlier, it is often the skill of the trainer which produces the training result, rather than the training material.

Pre-training assessment

The three principal stages of assessment which will be covered here – Pre-Training, During Training and End of Training – all reflect the three major aspects of training – Knowledge, Skills and Attitudes.

Knowledge
Unless the subject is specialized trainees will have some knowledge of the subject prior to a training course. This will certainly be true of the more mature learner, or those who are already employed in the company, industry or industry sector. It may be less likely if new entrants to the job, company or industry and sector are involved. Learners should therefore be tested before training so that the effectiveness of the training can be assessed. Both oral and written tests are available, although some form of written rather than oral test is more usual.

Open answer
Probably the commonest form of test of knowledge or examination is where questions are set so that there is no clue to the answer. Typical examples of this approach are:

Compare the advantages and disadvantages of . . .
Discuss the effects of 'x' on subject 'y' during the period 'z'.

Two main problems are found with this type of test:

1. The question has to be set in such a way that it is completely understandable in exactly the same way by all the persons being tested. There is little value if the question is seen to be asking different things by several different people.
2. The answers will be given, usually in open text, in the style and to the extent determined by the responder. Consequently, if 20 people are asked to complete the question, the responses will be almost certainly given in 20 different ways – construction,

grammar, spelling, content, etc. All of these will need to be assessed and compared with a set standard.

If the test is repeated at the end of the training, the improvement in responses will give indications of the effectiveness of the training; they are less likely to reflect the effectiveness of the trainer.

Binary choice questions

Rather than asking for open answers, with the resulting difficulties summarized above, binary choice questions can be set. The simplest forms of these set a question and offer a choice between two responses – usually either YES/NO, or short phrases. An example of this type of test would be:

(Delete inappropriate answer)

1. Does your company offer annual appraisal interviews?

    YES/NO

2. How effective does the company report state that these appraisals are?

    VERY
    EFFECTIVE/INEFFECTIVE

3. Does the annual company report state whether these appraisals are wanted by the employees?

    YES/NO

Such a technique is very limited, but the questions can follow a progressive line in relation to the training given. The benefits of this type of test are that:

*   The questions can be related to earlier stages of the training;
*   The marking/scoring is much easier than assessing open answers;
*   Consistent 'correct' answers can be agreed upon before the training.

There are fairly specific rules which must be followed else the test will lose some of its objectivity:

*   The choice of language must be careful to prevent ambiguous questions. This is not as easy as it sounds. Take for example, question 1 above; would everybody understand the word 'offer' in exactly the same way, or would some people interpret it in a different way, and would some people have doubts as to what exactly was meant?
*   The question posed must be singular, that is it must consist of one part only to prevent confusion. The intention here is to determine the extent of the knowledge of the learner, not to test any other skills they may have.
*   One of the answers given in the binary choice must be correct and there must be no ambiguity or doubt about its correctness.

True/false choice questions
Like the Binary Choice approach, the test offers a choice of two answers, but here it is between True and False. For example,

A red light signifies that the
machine is in operation. TRUE/FALSE? (Put a stroke through the incorrect answer)

   This test must follow the same guidelines given for the Binary Choice and has the similar advantage of simplicity of scoring, but it also suffers from the same disadvantage in that the learner may be tempted to guess the answers, having a fifty-fifty chance of them being correct. The total response will follow the Law of Probability, although the test is intended to assess real knowledge.

Multiple choice questions
One way of avoiding the problem of guesswork contaminating the real knowledge level is to offer a number of choices. The number of choices usually ranges between three and five, although it can be readily extended to seven. A 'silly' answer is often included in the list, although if the answer is too silly there seems to be little reason for its inclusion. A typical five-choice question could be:

(Ring the number of the answer you think is the correct one)
   The company's annual Job Appraisal Review Interview is
   1. Mandatory for all staff
   2. Mandatory for all staff from Supervisor level up
   3. Voluntary for all staff
   4. Voluntary for all staff up to the age of 60
   5. Voluntary for all staff over the age of 60?

   The multiple choice test is more difficult to construct than the previous examples because of the need to produce a number of alternatives for each question, but scoring or marking is simple against a 'correct' score sheet.
   The example quoted above is one variation of this type of test – the 'incomplete answer' test, because one of the alternatives offered completes the sentence correctly. An alternative approach is to have the stem of the test as the question, although still offering alternative choices. For example:

What are the recommended tyre pressures for a Zuba 327SLGi?
1. $28lb/in^2$ front and rear
2. $30lb/in^2$ front and rear
3. $28lb/in^2$ front, $30lb/in^2$ rear

4. 30lb/in² front, 28lb/in² rear
5. 40lb/in² front and rear?
(Please ring the number of the statement you think is correct)

Open short answers
Another test is one in which a statement is given which is incomplete. To complete the statement, the learner has to supply a short answer. In some cases this might be one word or figure;

> The minimum stopping distance for a car travelling at 40mph in dry road conditions is . . .

In other cases, the learner may have to give a short explanation in his own words. Although the answers may not be capable of being scored as quickly as the tests where a choice of answers is given, the responses to questions in this kind of test are usually sufficiently short to be scored quickly. This is a recommended form of testing, because, like the open, examination type of test, the responder has to know the answer and be capable of expressing it, the responses are not the problem which the open question marker faces. The responses to this type of test can demonstrate rather more than simple rote learning and consequently give an indication of the training quality.

Skills

Skills are the practical outcomes of knowledge, understanding and the ability to put them into practice, whether they are already held or have been acquired through training. Consequently tests of skill are required in training whenever a trainee (or control group member) needs to be able to translate learning into practice. Such tests may include those to measure:

- The *quality* of a finished task;
- The *accuracy* of a physical or mental operation (this will link directly with the knowledge tests to determine whether the trainee can *do* what he *knows*);
- The speed of task completion where speed is part of the task requirement;
- Completeness in performing the task (there is little value in performing a task perfectly if the whole task is not complete);
- Abilities in planning, organizing, communicating, designing, etc. (these may have been part of the training at the theoretical, model level – can the trainee put the model into real action, or, if pre-

testing, does the potential trainee have any idea what he is trying to do?

- competence in identifying correctly mechanical components, completed written procedures.

Interpersonal 'skills' are generally excluded from this list because the 'skills' are much more subjective and are much more difficult to measure.

Implementation of skills tests

Skills tests should be relatively easy to apply to trainees when they attend a training course, or prior to attempting a learning package, provided either a specific end product or a qualified observer is present to validate the skill. Often trainees attend the training because it has already been assessed at the workplace that they are unable to fulfil the necessary skill standards. It would be unwise for the trainer to agree to accept a trainee onto his course without testing whether the potential trainee has the skill to learn, and what level of *any* skill he possesses.

If control groups are involved in the pre-testing, the same assessment criteria must be applied to them as to the training group. If an assessment is to be accepted on the word of the person's immediate superior, this must be so of both groups. If a specific test is to be applied, and this is certainly recommended, then both the control and the training must follow this test under exactly the same conditions, and with the test facilitated by the trainer.

Construction of skills tests

Although there is as much, if not more, variety in skills testing as there is in knowledge testing, the construction of tests must follow a set of specific guidelines to ensure that the tests are valid – to be able to 'do' the task is simply not a sufficient test of competence and skill.

1. The skills test must be directly related to the training terminal objective. There is always a great temptation for trainers to set high skills standards to see whether the trainees can cope with more than is essentially necessary. If the trainee proves this, so what? If every trainee shows that they are capable of more than the terminal objective for this task, either the training population is the wrong one, the training task has been set at too low a level, or there is no need for the training and the training needs analysis has been faulty. One expression which is often used in training is 'Why give Rolls Royce training when Mini training is all that is required'!

2. The test, and the terminal objective, must be completely accurate and accepted within the occupation and the organization. The ter-

minal objective will have an end product, but other actions will precede it. Similarly in the test. If the test is one of accountancy procedure, in real work practice experienced workers cut corners to save time and energy. The terminal objective must ensure that these short cuts are not trained for – if subsequently the 'organization' permits them, well and good, but training must follow the recognized, safe, complete path. In the same way the test must be designed and/or scored on the basis that a certain procedure has to be followed.

3. The instructions for the test, the skill level possible, the time available and any other factors should be completely clear and unambiguous and every effort should be made to ensure that the potential trainee or control group member understands what they have to do. It is also valuable at the pre-training stage to let the testees know that they are not necessarily expected to complete the test, and that it is principally intended to determine their *level* of skill.

4. The trainers must ensure, as far as possible, that before the first occasion on which the test is used that it is a valid test and will not need modifications for further use. Otherwise different groups will be unfairly tested with different instruments, however small the modification may be. The tests must be presented in exactly the same way on each occasion, irrespective of who is presenting them. It is valuable to have a written briefing, which itself has been validated, which can be either read by the testees or, preferably, read to them by the tester.

5. The test environment should replicate the conditions under which the skill is to be performed; often the best place is in the workplace itself. Situational realism is highly desirable when emergency skills are being considered, but often modifications have to be made or simulations introduced to avoid dangerous situations. This, of course, was the principal reason for the development of the flight simulator in the training of aircraft pilots.

6. The scoring, marking or assessment system must be standardized so that different testers will not assess in different ways. The test must avoid the dangers of accepting that the testee 'was about to do that anyway'.

7. Ensure that the test, at least for the terminal objective testing, has a realistic but challenging performance criterion. I have seen too many training objectives which require the trainee to show in the final test a competence level of 75 or 80 per cent. Some tasks require 100 per cent competence – would you be happy about flying with a pilot who had achieved 85 per cent competence? What if the remaining 15 per cent competence was needed on an occasion when he was flying the aircraft on which you were a passenger? Or the welder, who is required to achieve a 90 per cent competence level. If the object you were using had been welded failed because

of that 10%, would you be in a position to complain? These are obviously 'life and death' situations, but even though a task is not of this order, there is little justification in not aiming for 100 per cent success at the end of the training programme. Settling for less is accepting that the training is less than 100 per cent itself.

Subjective skills

It is much more difficult to design, apply and score tests for the more subjective 'skills' than for the mechanical, systems, procedural, etc. task skills. In the latter there are absolute standards which can be applied so that the results can be validated with a reasonable amount of accuracy. When we start talking about other kinds of skills however, many more difficulties of assessment appear.

Take, for example, the case of an intended course of training for managers in negotiating skills. The pre-tests could take various forms. The manager's manager might make the statement that his subordinate 'needs to be better at negotiating'. Attempts to elucidate this statement in quantitative terms are often doomed to failure. The question can be asked 'Why do you say he "needs to be better"?'. The responses can range from the almost impossibly subjective 'Oh, I just think he does' to an apparently objective statement that he 'failed' in his last six negotiations. Behind this latter statement there may be many more reasons than lack of skill, although that may in fact be the prime consideration. It may be that the last six negotiations he had to perform were impossible ones in which to succeed; a number of back-up conditions did not support his negotiating; the power base in the negotiation gave him no chance of succeeding, and so on. What there are are usually indications of a training need which have to be investigated in as many ways as possible.

Pre-testing subjective skills

The first requirement has to be the acceptance by the tester that the methods of assessing subjective skills will almost certainly themselves be subjective and the results will be open to challenge. This being accepted, it is usually necessary to approach the pre testing in a number of ways. Certainly the views of the individual's superior(s) must be taken into account, and also the views of the potential trainees themselves – whether by interview response, self-assessment inventory and/or track record determined in some way.

It is rare that the 'tester' will have the opportunity to observe the individual actually in situ. The next best trial situation will be at the start of the course with a simulation. In the skill area we are discussing this would be a simulated negotiation, either with the training staff or with fellow course members, under the observation of the training staff.

Even these assessments must be necessarily subjective because any assessment will have to be made against a model standard accepted by the trainer and the organization. Does the organization require win/lose or win/win negotiators? This will make a difference to the initial assessment, the training course and the terminal objectives. How capable are:

1. The senior managers of making assessments of skill
2. The potential trainee of making a self-assessment (and against which criteria)?

In the case of 2., I have determined an approach (known as the Three-Test) which will be referred to later as reducing the subjectivity of self-assessment.

The most the trainer can hope for at this stage is an amalgamation of 'views' and self-views which cumulatively will help to build up a picture of the potential trainee's apparent 'skill'. It is helpful if any tests given at this stage are repeated at the end of the training – they may not be accurate, but at least they are roughly comparable. The problem is that really the live assessors – the trainees' managers – may not have any better criteria against which to assess the individual once he has been trained. Assessment in these cases is very difficult, perhaps impossible, but I believe that attempting 'something' is considerably better than doing nothing at all.

Attitude pre-testing

If the approach to skills testing in some areas is difficult, attempting to do the same for attitudes is even more so. Attitudes and behaviour are completely subjective, objectivity being approached only by models based on existing cultures. Even so these cultures change over periods of time, from country to country, from 'class' level to 'class' level and from individual to individual. Any organization which involves itself in attitudes training, and here the borders between attitudes and skills are very hazy, must define exactly what attitudes and behaviour it will treat as the norm of the organization. This is made even more difficult at the present time when relationships, negotiations and other forms of contact are increasingly being made between cultures whose values and attitudes have to be considered. Business approaches between western and eastern cultures have to be tailored to these differences; even approaches within Europe have some areas of sensitivity. Consequently, when we are trying to assess the effectiveness of attitude training, the base model, however subjective, must be clear.

Apart from the subjective appraisal of individuals by their managers,

ELLRAY ASSOCIATES
BEHAVIOUR SKILLS QUESTIONNAIRE

NAME_____   DATE_____

Please enter a tick alongside each item on the scale 1 to 10 representing where you consider your present level of skill might be.

LOW   HIGH
1 2 3 4 5 6 7 8 9 10

1. Being aware of my
    own behaviour
2. Being aware of the
    reaction of others
    to my behaviour
3. Being aware of the
    behaviour of others
4. Being aware of my
    reactions to the
    behaviour of others
5. Being aware of how
    much I talk
6. Being aware of how
    much I support
    others
7. Being aware of how
    much I build on
    others' ideas
8. Sensing the feelings
    of others
9. Being aware of how
    much I interrupt
    others
10. Being aware of how
    much I really listen
    to others
11. Telling others what
    my feelings are
12. Being aware of what
    behaviour modification
    I need to do
13. Knowing how to modify
    my behaviour
14. Being aware of how
    much I bring out the
    views of others.

1 2 3 4 5 6 7 8 9 10

Figure 7.1 Behaviour self-assessment questionnaire

most of the pre-tests for attitude aspects are based on self-assessment inventories. These are notoriously subjective and open to distortion, deliberate or unconscious. Again, if it is at all possible, assessments at this stage must be validated as far as possible by multiple assessments.

The observational technique known as Behaviour Analysis, a very useful form of activity analysis, can be invaluable at this stage if:

1. A qualified observer is available to use the analysis
2. Time is available to perform the analysis.

This technique will be described later.

Self-assessment

The most common form of assessment for attitude rating is the use of some form of self-assessment inventory. It has been mentioned earlier that if self-assessment is used in the simple, classical pre- and post-test approach, severe discrepancies can result, but these can be minimized by the Three-Test method (see page 113). The format of the self-assessment inventory will depend on the area of attitude training being considered. If this is, for example, Interpersonal Skills, a typical questionnaire might be that shown in Figure 7.1.

It will be apparent that the methods for assessing various types of training are many and varied. Although there is not necessarily one approach for each type of training, different tests are more effective with certain types of training. Each training event must be evaluated to determine the most appropriate and effective form of validation.

8

Ongoing assessment

The main purpose of validation is to determine the change in knowledge, skills and/or attitudes as a result of the training. During training events lasting longer than three days, it is advisable to maintain an ongoing validation of the effectiveness of the training. Without it (and its occurrence is by no means universal, sometimes for valid time and resource reasons), it can suggest that:

- The trainer is not interested in the progress of his training (and therefore is not an effective trainer);
- The trainees and their needs are being ignored;
- The training may be proceeding in a completely ineffective way.

The interim validation need not be a major operation, occupying usually only a short period of time each day, although there are some approaches which are much more complex and require more time. It is crucial that:

- The feedback given by the trainees is listened to by the trainers;
- Sufficient time is given to show that the operation is an important aspect of the training;
- The trainer has the authority to act upon any feedback.

If *all* these criteria are not followed, interim validation has little value and any efforts will reveal the trainer to be ineffective.

Session and daily validation

The simplest form of interim validation is a constant check on progress after each session or day during the course or event. The approaches are virtually the same as the pre-training techniques of knowledge, skills and attitudes.

In the case of knowledge training, tests can be applied at relevant intervals, the content based on the stage of learning which should have been achieved by that time. These tests should preferably be of the same nature as the pre-training tests.

Skills training, whether of mechanical objective or subjective skills, can similarly produce interim validation tests and inventories, like those we discussed in the pre-training stage.

In the more general areas of skills training, it is usual to have some form of questionnaire completed after a particular training session or at the end of a training day, in an attempt to check out that the learners have progressed sufficiently along the determined training path.

As suggested this can be in the form of a practical test, or if this is not the type of training involved, a questionnaire based on the material which has been presented and should have been learned. The type of questionnaire will be considered later, but the timing of these approaches can be critical.

If the training is divided into specific sessions which are complete units in themselves, testing can be carried out with validity after each session. One danger is that learners might react against the over-use of tests and questionnaires, making them counterproductive.

Many general training events do not have sessions which are strictly defined. If the validation is completed immediately after the session, the principal advantage is that the learners will not have had any opportunity to forget whatever they learned from the session; neither will they have had the opportunity to reflect on the lessons presented, particularly if the learning preference of the individual is 'Reflective' and the training has perhaps been a complex activity.

The principal disadvantage is when the sessions are not unique or self-contained. Many courses use an input session, followed by an activity, followed by a discussion, followed perhaps by a video, then a final discussion, all on the same topic. The session alone may not have made much impact on the learners and perhaps they could not even see the importance or significance of the material. If a validation questionnaire is completed after the session in such circumstances, the comments would probably be far from favourable. At the end of the complete sequence however, all the elements start to combine together to make a lot of sense and the learners would have a better opportunity of realizing the value of the session. That would be the stage when completion of a validation instrument would have the most relevance.

Many training courses of several days duration have a theme which runs for a complete day. In such cases, the end of the day is the most appropriate time to ask the learners to consider and report on the day's work. This can take several forms, usually either a verbal report-back or the completion of individual reactionnaires.

If the feedback is to be verbal, care must be taken as to how this is approached. The most straightforward method is for the trainer to present the training group with a set of verbal or flipchart-presented questions about the learning, or even more simply to ask them what they have learned/thought about the day's training. The report-back is taken immediately with the whole training group, in theory so that everybody with anything to say can do so and be supported or contradicted by other members of the group. In practice, the comments are made by the strongest/most vocal/most articulate members of the group and their views may not represent the views of whole. My experience, suggests that on such occasions, when there are one or two dominant contributors in the group, these are usually the ones who want to demonstrate their 'superiority' and challenge many aspects in an obstructive way.

One way to avoid bias is to give the group a set of questions about the day's training and ask them to write down their views. Once the views are written down, the open forum described above has a greater chance of hearing the opinions of the quieter members because they have something written on which to base their contributions – often a necessary aid for introverted people.

Many trainers divide the training group into smaller sub-groups and ask them to go into syndicate, to produce the small-group view of the day's training, and to appoint a reporter from each sub-group. At the report-back stage the views of each group are given by the reporters, who need not necessarily agree with the views they are presenting. What is being presented are the views of the majority. There is always the chance that the stronger members have dominated the sub-groups, but if an opportunity is given, after the reporter has made the group statement, for individuals to add anything, because they have already spoken in the small groups, the quieter members may be more likely to contribute if they disagree with the report.

Last thing/first thing?

Is it better to have the comments about a day's training immediately at the end of the day, or the next morning? If the training group is given overnight to reflect on the learning with or without an aiding questionnaire, they will have had time to form an opinion. There is, however, the opposite view that by the time the next morning comes, unless it is a very contentious issue, they may feel that the previous day is history and they want to get on with the new day's training.

Whichever approach is adopted the trainer must:

- Allow sufficient time for discussion and comment;
- Be prepared to give time to clear any problems which may have arisen from the feedback.

It is often very useful for an assessor of the trainer to sit in on these feedbacks, provided that his presence is not seen as an inhibitory factor. If a number of points fed back to a particular trainer require clarification of some aspects of the training, this is very significant in an assessment of the trainer's skill. Such feedback must be taken as a pointer only, to be supported by other forms of assessment.

A progressive interim validation

If the training has been particularly complex and the trainer wishes to assess the learning, repeating needs, and areas of omission, and is prepared to make a reasonable amount of time available, there is at least one approach which is a useful extension of the simple feedback. The purpose of this approach, which can occupy at least an hour, is to give the learners the opportunity to discuss the training event so far in as much detail as they wish, to compare their views with those of others, then make decisions on the main areas on which they require some action. The end result of this method is sometimes simply that everything has been understood and is going well. There is no problem here because the trainer or assessor needs to know when things are going right as well as when they are going wrong. A complete endorsement is rare, particularly in the difficult subject areas where there are no right and wrong answers.

Let us take a group of 16 learners, not an unusual size for a training event, although the approach can be used with smaller numbers. Ten is about the minimum, but below this the approach can still be applied with some modifications.

The training group is asked firstly as individuals to identify and write down for their own use 'three significant statements' they would like to make about the event so far. This wording does not direct the learners to look at any specific aspect, good or bad, but gives them the opportunity to express a view on whatever they find important to them. Once the individual statements have been produced, the group is divided into eight pairs and asked to produce, between each pair, an agreed three significant statements from the six they will be bringing to the pair.

When the pairs have reached their conclusions, groups of four are formed – in this case, four groups. Six statements produced by the two pairs are brought to each group of four and they are invited to refine these six into three statements.

At this stage there may be variations in the grouping. The four groups can be grouped into two sets of eight to produce two sets of three statements. Or the four groups can be brought into one group of 16 and asked to agree on six statements from the 12 they will bring with them. Whichever path is followed, the objective is to have six statements which obviously have been discussed, argued over, negotiated and agreed upon.

The six statements, which will be of value in assessing the progress of the training, can then be listed on a flipchart with four columns to the right of the statements. The four columns can be headed 'Strongly Disagree' (or SD), 'Disagree' (or D), 'Agree' (or A) and 'Strongly Agree' (or SA), as demonstrated in Figure 8.1.

ELLRAY ASSOCIATES

DURING-COURSE VALIDATON

STATEMENT	SA	A	D	SD

Figure 8.1   Interim validation

The learners are then invited to come to the flipchart and mark the column against each statement with their personal views. For example, a tick, cross or asterisk could be used to enter these views in the relevant column – SD, D, A, SA. The resulting pattern will certainly indicate the significant views of the group and also show the numbers of those who are not with the majority. A discussion can then follow about the results, and the trainer *must* then take action to satisfy the stated needs of the learners.

Objective observation assessment

In certain types of training event which are behaviourally anchored, the trainer can make an observational assessment of the progress and problems of the learners. If there are a number of activities, during the training which enable the learners to demonstrate their learning of the techniques, etc. observation may be fairly simple. The actions and behaviours of the learners in these activities can be assessed against an accepted and acceptable model of progress. Much of this assessment will be subjective. Even the model on which the observation is based may have highly subjective base values.

Behaviour analysis

Interaction analysis attempts to move away from the subjectivity of observation. Behaviour Analysis is a form of interaction analysis which is simple to operate and which can be modified to suit a number of different types of learning events – interpersonal skills, interview training of various types, negotiation training, sales training, etc. The variation for the event is introduced by changing the 'categories' of observation.

The more usual use of Behaviour Analysis (BA) is in the observation of verbal behaviours amongst individuals in groups, and of the behaviour of the groups themselves. Naturally, the range of possible behaviours which can occur within any group is considerable and the number of likely categories of behaviour would make the analysis observation impossible. There are, however, a number of commonly occurring behaviours and amongst these are a smaller number of behaviours which, if inappropriate, can be rectified by the person exhibiting them. Consequently there is sense in observing behaviours which can be modified, rather than simply observing behaviours.

Neil Rackham, Peter Honey and others were the initiators of this particular form of interactive analysis and they produced a set of behaviour categories, which are described in Figure 8.2.

DEFINITIONS OF BEHAVIOUR ANALYSIS CATEGORIES

Proposing	Putting forward a new concept, suggestion or proposal for positive action, often signalled by 'I propose/suggest that . . .', 'I think we should . . .', 'Let's . . .'. The more acceptable form of proposing may be to couch it in questioning terms e.g. 'What do you think about us doing . . . ?', rather than in the form of the statement. Proposals can come in a variety of forms which may need to be identified – Procedure Proposals, Content Proposals, Accepted Proposals, Lost Proposals etc.
Building	Extends or develops a proposal made by someone else, thus increasing its value. E.g. 'Let's go to the cinema' [Proposal]; 'Yes. Let's go to the Odeon because there's a horror film on there and we all like horror films' [Building].
Seeking information, views, feelings, suggestions.	A questioning behaviour intended to obtain specific responses from another. [Questions can be phrased in a variety of ways – some effective, others generally not so effective].
Seeking ideas	Specifically asking for proposals or suggestions to be made.
Giving information, views, feelings, opinions.	Statements made by the contributors about their views, opinions, feelings or giving information. Sometimes it can be difficult to differentiate between a statement and a proposal, particularly when the contribution is made in a confused or vague manner.
Disagreeing with reasons.	A statement where the contributor disagrees with a proposal or statement made by another, but where the reasons for disagreement are stated fully.
Supporting	A conscious, direct and positive declaration of support for a proposal or statement made by another.
Open	Usually an admission of guilt, or error, or inadequacy, made in a conciliatory rather than a defensive manner. Can be a simple statement 'I'm sorry'.
Summarizing	A behaviour particularly appropriate, though not exclusively, to a leader, where a full and accurate summary of what has transpired to that stage is given.
Attacking/Defending	A behaviour where one person, overtly, verbally, 'attacks' another by the emotional use of words or tone of voice. E.g. 'I might have expected you to say that' would probably be perceived as an attack on one's value judgements and would probably lead to a counter-attack or the taking of a defensive stance.
Blocking	Contributions which add nothing to the discussion or place a block or difficulty in the path

93

of the discussion, and are usually bald statements. E.g. 'Oh, we're just going around in circles' may be correct but it does nothing to help the group forward. Facetious remarks, particularly when they become frequent have the same effect.

Bringing-in   A direct and conscious attempt to involve another person, usually inviting them by name. It is invariably linked with 'Seeking'. In BA two contributions are scored – one for the bringing-in and the other for seeking.

Shutting-out   An attempt, successful or otherwise, noticed or ignored, to exclude others. It can be by:
- interrupting another before they have finished speaking
- side-talking when the rest of the group is discussing something
- coming in when someone else has been invited to speak.

As with 'bringing-in', two contributions should normally be scored – one for the interruption and the other for whatever contribution is made by the shutter-out [if this can be heard].

Figure 8.2   Behaviour Analysis categories

Using a specially designed BA sheet with the categories entered and columns for the participants, the number of occurrences of each category of behaviour against each participant can be logged and a pattern of behaviour identified.

It will be apparent that this approach is eminently suitable for certain occasions when a trainer is being observed for assessment. We shall return to this later.

Feelings reviews

The final type of interim review to be described is one related to assessing the feelings of the learners. Although it is directly aimed at encouraging *feelings*, at the same time the attitudes and views of the learners about the training, the trainer and any other aspect can emerge.

There are a variety of ways of using this type of approach. My favourite way, particularly useful on interpersonal skills events, is to offer a 'feelings review' at the start of each morning from the second day onwards.

The individuals of the learning group are asked to write down three words or short phrases which express their feelings at that moment. No other directions are given on the basis that the main feelings which emerge will almost certainly be about the event. After obtaining the group's permission, the feelings of each learner are listed on a flipchart. Once all the words and phrases have been posted, the group is asked whether any member wishes to say anything about their choice of words or phrases, or whether any other member wishes to ask the others about the words, etc. The trainer will stop any discussion until all the entries have been made and then gently question some of the group (without 'picking on' any) about their choice of words.

The trainer, particularly on the second and subsequent uses of the approach, must be prepared for a serious, often lengthy, often emotional discussion in which he is often deeply involved. Care must be taken that if certain feelings emerge in a number of learners, expressing doubt or hesitancy about something which has happened but will not be covered again, the trainer must take whatever action might be necessary to allay any fears or problems.

If a constant check is maintained by the trainer during the progress of a training event, and action is taken to remedy any deficiency discovered by any of the interim reviews, there is a greater likelihood that the training will be a success, not only because of the training content, but because of the effectiveness and concern of the trainer.

Training validation inventories

The three stages of training validation – pre-, interim and end-of-training assessments – are all equally important and should be made if the validation approach is to mean anything. However, for a variety of reasons – lack of resource, lack of time, disinterest, lack of knowledge and skill, etc. – frequently all these steps are not taken. Most often some attempt is made at training validation at the end of the course. Even so, validation is rarely given the time and attention it deserves.

The principal purpose of end-of-course validation is to:

1. Check whether the terminal objectives initially included in the course design have been fully or partially achieved;
2. Assess whether there has been any change in knowledge, skills and/or attitudes of the learners (obviously if this hasn't been assessed prior to the training, end-of-course validation is very much a waste of time).

One factor in the equation of success or failure of the training is the role of the trainer in the process. The validation of the *training*, as we saw earlier, will give very strong leads to this assessment.

95

Knowledge

The knowledge tests provided for the end-of-training validation will be very similar to those used in pre-training and interim validation. Preferably, the same tests should apply for the pre-test and for the post-test. The interim tests will frequently be staged depending on the nature of the training.

The post-training tests, used in both the training and the control groups, must be applied scrupulously. They may reveal a wide range of gains in knowledge across the training group. It is too easy to accept the ones who do satisfactorily in the test as having benefited from the training, whereas the ones who do not do as well are considered to have 'failed' because of the type of people they are – remember the earlier quote 'That was a good course. That was a bad group'? If some of the learners do not perform in the test as well as the terminal objectives require, the following questions must be asked:

- Was the material the correct material?
- Was the training presented in the most appropriate way?
- Was the training provided the most appropriate approach?
- Was the training material broken down into sufficiently digestible steps?
- Was the training material clear?
- Did the trainers check progress during the training?
- To what extent did the trainer present the training material in the most efficient and effective manner?

Skills

Validating the learning of practical skills is generally as simple as testing of pre-training practical skills and knowledge as described above. Skill is the practical application of knowledge, thus demonstrating understanding. The potential gas meter reader who prior to the training had no knowledge or skills in reading meters can be checked by a practical test to see whether he has satisfied the prescribed terminal objectives. Can he read the number of gas meters required, to the required accuracy, within the prescribed time, exhibiting the appropriate attitudes? If so, the learner and the training have been successful. If not, the training has failed to achieve the objectives with that learner – why? The questions listed above will need to be asked.

Subjective skills and attitudes

When we try to assess whether the training objectives have been met, whether the learner has progressed, and whether the training has been validated, we meet the same problems we encountered with pre-testing. We are forced to rely on subjective assessments to reach any conclusions at all.

The use of questionnaires to answer subjective questions is widespread. The number of questionnaires or reactionnaires used by many trainers on many courses suggests that we have attained a high level of skill and success with this approach. This is not the case, as is evident from the questionnaires highly derogatory title of 'happiness sheets' given to end-of-course questionnaires, many of which are designed to ensure that a good rating is given for the training and the trainer. The questionnaire is completed in an obvious air of euphoria, and neither the trainer nor the learners give it the importance it deserves. It is in the interest of all trainers completing a training programme and all training managers or others who are responsible for assessing the affectiveness of training and the competence of trainers to ensure the end-of-course validation measures they are using are fully effective. Even these reveal that there are some problems. The most ineffective trainers are those who either continue training without modification, even though they know that training is not achieving its objectives, or those who are not aware of whether or not the training is effective.

The variety of end-of-course validation instruments is extremely wide, and there will be room here to describe only one or two of these. There are three important factors when asking learners to complete an end-of-course questionnaire or other inventory:

1. Sufficient time must be allocated in the training programme for the learners to reflect on the training they have received – decide what they wish to say about it and comment to a greater extent than simply placing a tick on a list.
2. The questionnaire must be constructed in such a way that any undue bias is avoided.
3. Emphasis must be placed by the trainer on the importance of the assessments (to the training event, to the trainer, to themselves because the assessment will be used within the continuing evaluation, and to future learners who will be attending the programme). Information must also be given about what will happen to the completed inventories, who will see them and how they will be used.

There is some argument as to whether the terminal validation questionnaire should be completed at the end of the course, or taken away by the learner for completion back at work and sent back to the trainer. If the questionnaire is completed at the end of the course:

- It may be completed in an atmosphere of euphoria or frustration, depending on factors which may have had nothing to do with the learning;
- Because the learners are ready to leave the event, they may not be able to give sufficient attention to reflect on what has happened and to assess the significant points.

I have found that both these arguments cancel each other out when the points described above are followed. Once the validation is seen as part of the event, there is a greater likelihood that the learners will give it the attention which they gave to the rest of the training. The apparent advantages are that:

- The training is fresh in the mind of the learners.
- Completion before the learners leave the training environment ensures 100 per cent receipt of the assessments.

The benefits quoted for the delaying of completion until the learner has returned to work include:

- The opportunity is given for the learners to translate their training/-learning into the real work situation.
- Realistic completion of the inventory away from the atmosphere of the training event.
- The opportunity to reflect on the learning, its impact, its recall and its validity in the minds of the learners.

These are strong arguments, but can be only really acceptable for validation purposes if the questionnaires are in fact returned for analysis. Those that are not returned may be the most important ones. Unless the organization has a system for ensuring the return of the questionnaires, there is a very great danger that much less than 100 per cent response will result. Many trainers consider a response rate of 33 to 50 per cent as very good, and it is only the ones who can follow up or enforce the return who achieve almost a 100 per cent response rate.

A low response rate must be one of the problems of this approach. Another problem is that when the learners return to their work space they find so much work awaiting them that they become so immersed in catching up that the validation inventory loses any priority it may have had. The managers of learners are often to blame for this by not ensuring that they show interest in the training event by a debriefing interview and fail to ensure that any post-training requirements are met.

The compromise, of course, which can benefit the training validation is that the learners are asked to complete a questionnaire before they leave the training event (always bearing in mind the effectiveness criteria). A week or so after the event, the learners are sent the same questionnaire and asked to complete it and return it, taking into consideration the reflection they will have had since the end of the training. Some organizations require this follow-up questionnaire to be sent through the learner's manager, thus ensuring a much greater likelihood of completion and return.

Constructing questionnaires

A large number of rules, on the construction of valid questionnaires exists, based on sound psychological principles. Unless it is possible to assign the construction of a questionnaire to an expert in this field, it is most unlikely that the questionnaire used will satisfy all these requirements. There are one or two simple guidelines, however, which will help the non-specialist questionnaire constructor to produce a suitable format.

The first question to ask is 'What do I want to know?', followed very quickly by 'What do I need to know?'. It is so easy to be persuaded to include questions which would be nice to know. The criterion must be – 'Do I *need* to know?'.

The questions you ask must:

1. Differ from each other;
2. Be ones which the learners will be able to answer.

In the first case, if the question is constructed in such a way that it is clear and satisfies 2., there will be no need to repeat the question in different words, as so often happens, 'to ensure that I get the correct answers'. Make the single question unambiguous and clear and you should receive all the information you require.

One factor to bear in mind at all times is that the shorter the questionnaire, the shorter the list, the better the response, especially if the questionnaire is to be completed after the event. Brevity does not obviate the need for completeness, and in some situations, the list of questions included can be extensive.

Since the learners must be able to answer them,

1. The questions must relate to material which has been included in

the training programme (it is not the intention of the questionnaire to test the total range of the learner's knowledge).

2. The questions must be couched in language which will be understood without difficulty by the learners, even if this means using, say, three words instead of one.

The questionnaire must start with instructions on its completion. These instructions must be clear and concise and be unambiguous in their construction. There is little value in knowing the type of information required if this is not supplied because the learner cannot understand what is being sought. It is not sufficient to request that the completer 'indicates' which response they prefer, if there is no instruction about *how* to indicate – a tick, cross, asterisk, circle or any other defined mark.

The order of the questions can have a strong influence on the types of responses. The general rule is to start with general questions and move to more specific ones, in exactly the same way you would progress if you were conducting an interview. There may be some value in posing the most important questions early in the questionnaire because there may be a better chance of these being answered fully, particularly in a long questionnaire, than those towards the end of the list.

Question format. Closed questions should be avoided as much as possible, priority being given to more open questions, again as you would tend to do in an interview. After all, if you ask a closed question, you may receive only a very limited answer and this will require you to ask yet another question, thus increasing the length of the questionnaire. An open question will give the opportunity of a more extended answer, but it will not necessarily guarantee that you will receive a full answer.

Precision. Like the instructions the questions must be clear, concise and unambiguous. Some words aid ambiguity and should be avoided because they will often mean different things to different people – such words can be 'often', 'frequently', 'extensively', 'most', etc. The questionnaire should use positive rather than negative questions, although again there will be occasions when this is the only form of question possible. Ask one question only in each question – if a question consists of multiple parts, the responder can be confused about how to answer, particularly if the parts contradict each other. For example the question 'Do you enjoy driving, and if so, which is your favourite car?' contains two completely separate questions. If I had to answer that question, my answer 'yes' or 'no' to the first part would have no relationship at all to my answer to the second part. This is an obvious case for two separate questions.

Leading questions must be avoided, otherwise the completer might gain the impression that you are attempting to manipulate their responses to those that you are wanting – and this is usually the reason for a leading question! Rather than ask 'Don't you feel that the appraisal should be given every six months?', the format is more appropriate as 'How often do you feel the appraisal should be made?' or even 'How often do you feel the appraisal should be made? – Every month/Every three months/Every six months/Annually? (place a ring around the interval you prefer).' The latter might be used when brevity of response is required although it has the disadvantage of suggesting that you are leading the response to one and one only of the alternatives given – of course, this is exactly what you *are* doing, but this is justifiable if these are the only alternatives.

Finally the use of personal pronouns. Use at all times the relevant personal pronoun, or personal possessive adjective – 'you', 'your', 'yours', 'my', etc. rather than 'one', one's' and so on. This will tell the completer that it is *his* or *her* views that are being sought.

If there is one central message in assessment, whether for training or the trainer, that message is continuity. Isolated assessments, do little more than provide some information, and certainly offer an incomplete, and sometimes erroneous assessment. Continuous assessment demonstrates the progressive nature of training and the skill of the trainer at the various stages. Interim validation must only be introduced if there is going to be the opportunity to take practical account of what emerges, particularly if it reveals that the learners have not understood or accepted what has happened up to that stage. If there is no opportunity or intention to take action as a result of the learners' comments, interim validation can be an unnecessary practice.

9

End-of-course questionnaires

Types of questionnaire

A wide range of questionnaires exists, varying from those which give a maximum amount of valuable information to those which give information in a misleading way.

The following questionnaires are a brief selection only. Most of them can be modified if needed. Each will give you some information about the validity of the training and also, sometimes by inference, sometimes directly, the effectiveness of the trainer.

The open questionnaire

The open questionnaire is probably the simplest form of end-of-course validation questionnaire, but can be the most valuable because it gives the learners the complete opportunity to say whatever they wish about the training and allied matters. It consists of a blank sheet of paper on which the learners are invited to comment on whatever they wish (Figure 9.1).

ELLRAY ASSOCIATES

MEASURING THE RESULTS.

Please make any comments which you feel are important or significant on any aspect of the seminar. You may wish to add your name.

Figure 9.1 The open questionnaire

The advantages of this type of questionnaire are that:

- It requires no construction of questions and so avoids directing or misdirecting the learners;
- Responsibility for the comments and which comments are made is passed to the learner;
- The format allows the learners to make comments on any matter they care to raise.

Disadvantages include:

- Comments may be made on subjects not related to the training (if desired, this can be avoided by asking the completers to make their comments only on matters relating to the training, however, some valuable information might be lost if this injunction is made).
- Comments may not be made on the aspects which are of the most interest to the trainer (the trainer must be prepared for this with this form of questionnaire which gives *all* responsibility for the comments to the learner). The omission of certain comments, which may have been anticipated by the trainer, may be highly significant. The trainer may have felt that these omitted aspects were very

important parts of the training content – the learners obviously did not think so. Alternatively, the trainer may have felt that his presentation of certain parts of the training were exceptionally good, although the learners again clearly did not agree.
- It is very difficult to correlate the views of a number of learners because many of them will comment on exclusive and different subjects.

Because of these disadvantages, this form of reactionnaire, although very good for assessing training, is less useful for assessing the trainer (other than indirectly through the training assessment) as it does not address specific questions which will identify the trainer skills.

The open-question questionnaire

The next step forward from the empty sheet is the open-question questionnaire, which directs the learners to certain areas, albeit fairly general, of the training programme. Figure 9.2 shows a typical example.

The questions included on the form can be varied depending on the type of programme, the information specifically required by the trainer, and so on. The main requirement of the form is that although questions are asked, they are open questions which will allow the learner to answer in any way he wishes, and at any length. At the same time this is an advantage *and* a disadvantage. Although the format is more directive than the previous questionnaire, the response – its content, extent, approach – is still in the hands of the learner. Whilst this gives the learner a free hand in his answers and avoids any suspicion of manipulation, the nature of the responses can be so wide and varied that correlation is very difficult. In Figure 9.2 the questionnaire is principally directed at the effectiveness of the training and the actions resulting from it, but, if desired, an additional question or questions can be included directed specifically at the learners' reaction to the trainer. A question of this nature could be:

To what extent did the trainer contribute to any learning you have achieved?

How was this managed?

ELLRAY ASSOCIATES

MEASURING THE RESULTS.

1. Which parts of the event did you find the most useful?

2. Which parts of the event did you find the least useful?

3. Are there any parts of the event you would omit? If so, which parts?

4. Is there anything you would wish to see added to the event? If so, what?

5. Which of your personal objectives were satisfied?

6. Which of your personal objectives were not satisfied?

7. Which aspects are you most likely to implement?

8. Any other comments?

Please add your name if you wish to do so.

Figure 9.2   The open question questionnaire

Semantic differential and scoring questionnaires

In this type of questionnaire scoring is possible, which presents the problem of possible over-reliance on the scoring by the analyst. Because numbers are generally used in this scoring, the result tends to look mathematical, with all the logic and discipline this implies. Unfortunately, any scoring is really highly subjective and must be treated as an indication only.

Three variations of the end-of-course validation questionnaire are commonly used.

The Thurstone Scale

Numerical, quasi-mathematical scoring scales are not needed here, for the method is similar to the binary method of knowledge testing discussed earlier.

The questions set are based on the whole course content. (Figure 9.3) The difference from the yes/no approach is that this scale gives the completer the choice between agreeing or disagreeing with the statements made. There will always be cases where the choice is not black and white which may give the completer the greatest difficulty in answering either A or D. To avoid this problem, when the questionnaire is issued comments must be made that 'A' = Agree, or agree more than you disagree; 'D' = Disagree, or disagree more than you agree.

A MANAGER'S RESPONSIBILITIES.

(RING EITHER 'A' OR 'D' AGAINST EACH STATEMENT)

1. A manager's first responsibility is the care of his staff   A   D

2. A manager's first responsibility is to his employer   A   D

3. A manager's first responsibility is to the objectives of the organization   A   D

4. A manager must be able to do all the jobs of his staff   A   D

5. A manager must know more than his staff   A   D

6. A manager is closer to his staff than he is to his own line manager   A   D

etc.

Figure 9.3 A Thurstone Scale questionnaire.

The Likert Scale

The Likert Scale overcomes the limitations of the Thurstone Scale by offering a wider range of options – the equivalent of the knowledge multi-choice test. Commonly five choices are given, although there is often argument about the middle choice which offers uncertainty or neutrality. Figure 9.4 uses the same statements as Figure 9.3, but with additional choices.

SA = strongly agree
A = agree

U = uncertain
D = disagree
SD = strongly disagree.

1. A manager's first responsibility is
    the care of his staff   SA A U D SD

2. A manager's first responsibility is
    to his employer   SA A U D SD

3. A manager's first responsibility is
    to the objectives of the organization   SA A U D SD

4. A manager must be able to do all the
    jobs of his staff   SA A U D SD

5. A manager must know more than his staff   SA A U D SD

6. A manager is closer to his staff than
    he is to his own line manager   SA A U D SD

    etc.

Figure 9.4   A Likert Scale questionnaire

Semantic differential scale

The most common scale in use is the one which uses a semantic differential at the poles on the scoring scale, with a range of scores divisions in between. For example, at one pole of the scale is the rating 'good' and at the opposite pole the rating 'bad'. In questionnaires using this type of scale, the learners are asked to rate various factors on the scale. A typical example of this is shown in Figure 9.5, the event being part of the assessment by the learners of a session on a negotiation skills course.

SESSION: NEGOTIATION TECHNIQUES

	6	5	4	3	2	1	
Learned a lot			x				Learned little
Enjoyed the session		x					Didn't enjoy the session
Understood everything			x				Understood nothing
Techniques were acceptable		x					Techniques were not acceptable

Figure 9.5   Semantic differential scale questionnaire

The individual completers are required to rate the sessions using the scale divisions, usually a minimum of three, although five, six or seven divisions are common. The completers are asked to place a mark (tick, cross, asterisk, etc.) in the relevant division to which a number has been allotted.

A useful numerical scoring basis for analysis is thus obtained, and a set of questions and scales can be used for each session, or any other item about which views are required.

There is often argument over the number of divisions on the scale. If there is an odd number of divisions, say seven, there will obviously be a middle division at four. The practical problem with the option to mark such a score is that it will tend to be treated as the easy way out, either giving an 'average' marking whatever that might mean, or, worse, as a position to mark if no decision can be made – both are 'safe' markings. If this attitude can be overcome, the division '4' can be treated simply as what it is, a scoring position between 3 and 5. This attitude is possible to instil, but with difficulty owing to the general widespread concept of a middle position as 'average'.

If only six positions are available for scoring, the completers are forced to be positive in their assessments, putting their scoring either on the 'satisfactory +' or 'satisfactory −' halves of the scale.

Consistency in the scoring numbering and in which extreme pole the 'good' aspect is placed is essential. It does not matter too much whether the '6' or the '1' is on the left or right sides of the scale, or whether 'good' is on the left and 'bad' on the right, or whether '6' is 'good' and '1' is 'bad' or vice versa. But the entries must be consistent throughout the questionnaire to avoid confusion. The more common custom, although not always adhered to, is to have the 'good' or positive comment on the left side of the scale, linked with the higher number, e.g. good = 6, bad = 1.

One of the problems with the semantic differential scale is that the use of numbers gives the scale mathematical credence, whereas it is really almost as subjective as 'yes, no, don't know, might be, might not be'. The scale has to be anchored with the polarized statements, which may be subjective say:

'Completely. . . . Not at all'
'To a very large extent. . . . Hardly at all'
'To a maximum extent. . . . To a minimum extent'

In practice, this may not present a problem because the divisions at the extremes are rarely used. Raters in many fields are reluctant to use the '7s' and the '1s' of a rating scale. This, of course, argues for the use of a scale with a greater number of divisions.

End-of-course assessments

Problems may arise in the scoring of semantic differential scales. The use of scores enables the numerical comparison to be made between course members and consecutive sessions or courses, but the numbers can become all-important to the trainer who may evolve complex analytical assessments of the questionnaires. It can also be too easy for the learners simply to allocate scores, whether or not they have given sufficient consideration to the ratings.

A typical example of part of an end-of-course validation questionnaire is shown in Figure 9.6. The complete questionnaire can give almost at a glance what appears to be a picture of the success of the training, but this cannot be confirmed in any way other than by accepting the subjective, arbitrary allocation of scores.

If time for the validation measures is limited, and this is usually the case, the approach can give at least an *indication* of success of the training, and hence indirectly the effectiveness of the trainer.

ELLRAY ASSOCIATES

MEASURING THE RESULTS

Place a mark — x,*,0 etc. in the division for which you wish to give the score.

A. *SESSION: THE SKILLS OF THE EFFECTIVE TRAINER*

		7	6	5	4	3	2	1	
Enjoyment	A Lot								Little
Usefulness	A Lot								Little
Content of session	Good								Poor
Extent of learning	A lot								Little

B. *SESSION: TRAINER TYPES*

Figure 9.6 An end-of-course validation questionnaire

More demanding validation

In order to try to avoid the problems of questionnaires giving a false impression ('happiness sheets'), some questionnaire designers, when faced with a basic inventory, add, under the scoring scales, a space headed 'Comments'. In my experience, comments included in this type of space are either rarely made or have little value. A better way is to use a questionnaire designed particularly to elicit worthwhile comments. An example of this is shown in Figure 9.7.

ELLRAY ASSOCIATES

MEASURING THE RESULTS

A. *SESSION: THE SKILLS OF THE EFFECTIVE TRAINER.*

(Please place a tick above the number you rate)

Learned a lot 7 6 5 4 3 2 1 learned little

If you have ticked the range 1 to 4, please say why you have scored at that level.

If you have ticked the range 5 to 7, please say how you intend to use this learning.

B. *SESSION: TRAINER TYPES*

etc.

Figure 9.7 An improved validation questionnaire

In this example, the scoring scales are retained, but there is space to add questions other than those relating to learning. However, the questionnaire designer must be very clear why these questions need to be asked. The main purpose of training is learning and it is that we need to validate. Many other factors that accompany the learning can be assessed without a questionnaire and do not add to the *validation* of the training. In this example, in addition to the basic rating scales two questions about the scoring are asked. If low scores are given the learner is asked to say why he/she feels that there has been little learning. (It may be that the material was too complex; not broken down into digestible amounts; not relevant; badly presented, etc. – none of which would be evident from the scoring alone.) The same question *could* be asked if the scoring is at the higher end of the scale, but this would certainly reflect a desire, real or not on the part of the trainer, to receive praise, and thus continue the myth of the 'happiness sheet'. Instead, if the ratings are good and learning has been achieved, this is all we need to know, other than *what the learner is going to do with his new learning*. If there has been learning its translation into the learner's working life is the next most important step in the learning cycle.

Some trainers, while agreeing with the principal behind this type of questionnaire, still feels that they wish to obtain information/ratings on other aspects of the training – enjoyment, length of sessions, visual aids and their use, the accommodation, and so on. There is only one strong argument against the inclusion of factors such as these, which in themselves are interesting/useful items of information, and that is that the more numerous the questions posed in a questionnaire, the less the likelihood of obtaining full and honest responses (there may even be a law of reducing value in inverse proportion to the number of questions asked!). If additional questions and scales are included, they should use the format in Figure 9.7. Never present a rating scale alone without also having specific questions requiring answers to justify the rating or the use of the rating.

A comprehensive validation questionnaire

Many of the criteria described so far can be combined when an extensive validation questionnaire needs to be used. In such cases there is every support for a varied approach, using different methods of obtaining and assessing information. An example is shown in Figure 9.8.

ELLRAY ASSOCIATES

'*OPTIONS FOR TRAINERS*' *SEMINAR*

1. DID YOU OBTAIN WHAT YOU HOPED FOR FROM THIS SEMINAR? *Please ring the relevant answer.*

YES   MORE THAN EXPECTED   LESS THAN EXPECTED   NO

2. WHOSE IDEA WAS IT THAT YOU SHOULD ATTEND THIS SEMINAR? *Please tick the relevant answer(s)*

No idea
Boss
Colleague
Subordinate
Yourself
Other?

3. HOW USEFUL DID YOU FIND THE FOLLOWING ACTIVITIES ON THE SEM-INAR? *Please ring the relevant score.*

	Little use					Lot of use
OPTIONS RELATING TO THE INTRODUCTORY SESSIONS		1	2	3	4	5

If you gave a rating 1, 2 or 3, please state why you have given this rating.

If you have given a rating 4 or 5, please state how you intend to implement this learning.

	Little use					Lot of use
THE VOLUNTEERS ACTIVITY		1	2	3	4	5

If you gave a rating 1, 2 or 3, please state why you have given this rating.

If you have given a rating 4 or 5, please state how you intend to use this learning.

4. *WHAT SPECIFIC CHANGES WOULD YOU SUGGEST TO ENHANCE THE EFFEC-TIVENESS OF THE COURSE?*

ETC.

5. *WHAT WAS/WERE THE MOST SIGNIFICANT EVENT(S) FOR YOU ON THE SEMINAR? (AND WHY?).*

6. WHAT HAVE YOU LEARNED FROM THE SEMINAR WHICH YOU INTEND TO PUT INTO PRACTICE ON YOUR RETURN TO WORK?

7. (Anwering this question is not mandatory!) Would you attend a seminar on a different subject with this presenter, Leslie Rae?

Figure 9.8   A comprehensive end-of-course validation questionnaire

The Three-Test

Before leaving end-of-course validation and its relationship to assessing the effectiveness of the trainer, I should like to return to a particular type of questionnaire that was introduced in Chapter Seven in relation to the Behaviour Self-Assessment Questionnaire (Figure 7.1): the Three-Test approach.

As we have seen, traditionally a test is given at the start of the training and repeated at the end of the training – the Pre- Post-Training Test. In knowledge and practical training programmes this is a suitable approach showing the change in the learner from 'can't do' to (hopefully) 'can do'. This approach is not suitable for assessing change in the more subjective training areas, and even the 'practical' areas where general skills are being considered. It is particularly inappropriate in such areas as human relations training, interpersonal skills, interviewing training and even what appear to be specific, objective skills such as negotiating, presentations and the like. Subjective views based on the models used can be expressed, but these can vary considerably depending on the base used for the 'expert' approach. In many cases the best that can be done is to ask the learners themselves to assess their own progress. These comments can be compared with the similarly subjective views of the trainer.

Figure 7.1 showed a behaviour self-assessment questionnaire which can be administered at the start of an interpersonal skills programme to obtain the views of the learners on how they assess their behavioural skills at that stage before training. Let us take one of the items on this questionnaire, which asks them to rate themselves on a scale of 1 to 10 (1 being Low) as to their 'Being aware of my own behaviour'. One learner might make an entry of 8 – this learner considers that he is quite aware of his own behaviour, but there may be one or two small points of which he is not aware, and that is why he has come on the programme.

At the end of the training programme, the same questionnaire is administered once again, in exactly the same format, but on this occasion the learners are asked to rate themselves as they see themselves at that stage, having been through the programme. The initial questionnaire has been retained by the trainer and is not made available at this time to the learner lest it influences his replies. On this second occasion, our learner might rate the question quoted above as '9'. This is the classical Pre- and Post-Test and suggests, although subjectively and from the learner's viewpoint only, that learning has increased by a factor of 10 per cent. This may be considered to be a low factor for a week long training programme which was designed for people whose interpersonal skills have been assessed by the managers as requiring improvement. The trainer might consequently feel disappointed in the low amount of change and consider that either the material used or his skills left something to be desired.

I suggest that immediately following the second completion, and without reference to either the first or second test, the learners are asked to complete the same questionnaire a third time. On this occasion they are required to complete the questionnaire as if they were completing it at the start of the training programme, but knowing what they now know about the subject of behaviour, appropriate behaviour, behaviour modification, behaviour categorization and its meaning, and so on. This suggests, and the learners are usually in agreement with this, that they did not really know where they stood at the beginning of the programme because they were not aware of the implications of interpersonal skills – the reason why they had come on the programme.

At the third completion, the learner might revise his rating for the beginning of the programme to '2'. As he now rates himself as at '9', the increase in self-assessed skill is 70 per cent rather than 10 per cent – a much more healthy change over the learning programme! This is still highly subjective, but it is much better than nothing at all.

Action planning

Assessment of the success of a training event, and thence by inference some indications of the effectiveness of the trainer, depends on the learner's commitment to put the learning into action, and on his/her acceptance of the learning and any new concepts that may have been put forward. If there appears to be little commitment to applying 'new' techniques, etc. this suggests that the material is so far out of touch with reality that it should not have been introduced (a fault in design and planning by the trainer), was so complex and incomprehensible that it is impossible to translate to the work situation (a fault in content design), or was not understood (a fault in the trainer's presentation and awareness).

If, however, the learners make firm commitments to put a number of aspects into operation, the training has been successful and the trainer must be given credit for this. If the action plans include the items which were initially identified by the trainer as the most significant learning items, and in consequence some extra effort was put into that part of the training, the trainer has obviously been successful in conveying his opinion of its importance.

Again, like 'happiness sheets', it is only too easy to lead the learners to include in their action plans the items that the trainer wants them to include, thus demonstrating his 'skill'. This is equally dishonest on the part of the trainer. The learners should be encouraged and given sufficient time to reflect on the training, consider which factors they have felt to be most important and significant to *them*, and commit themselves in writing and take some positive action. They may not include the factors that the trainer feels they should, either from the training content or from his own presentations, but if this is the case, it has to be accepted – this is what the learner must want. Or perhaps, the factor on which the trainer thought he was having such an impact may not have appeared in this way at all to the learner – a cause for reflection by the trainer!

My preferred style of action plan sheet is shown in Figure 9.9.

ELLRAY ASSOCIATES

ACTION PLANNING

What I intend to do	How I intend to do it	With what resources	By when

Figure 9.9 Action planning

The examples described here are but a few of the many approaches the trainer can take in attempting to validate the training, of whatever nature. Some are more valid, some more complex, some more valuable than others, but all set out to try to assess as objectively as possible, how effective the training has been from the learner's point of view. In doing so, we have seen that the competence of the trainer may also be reflected in the training ratings, although we need to ask more questions to define this accurately.

End-of-course validation can thus be developed into a realistic and effective approach, making the continuance of the 'happiness' epithet unjustifiable. But the trainer must stress the importance of validation, allocating sufficient time for forms to be completed a serious manner, and using a measure which itself demonstrates that the learners' views should be, and will be, considered.

10

Practical steps in trainer assessment

The preceding chapters have been intended as a gradually developing introduction to this stage of the book where we shall be looking at the steps which can be taken to answer the question 'How do we assess the effectiveness of a trainer?'. Even with the information we should already have, and other approaches which can and should be made, this is not going to be an easy task. A number of factors have to be taken into account, as well as the ways 'assessors' look at the direct actions of the trainer.

Initial steps in assessment

Firstly, as we saw in Chapter One, the place of the trainer within the training organization and the wider employing organization must be recognized – the Training Quintet which was described. His place in terms of authority, responsibility and hierarchy must be established to provide a base on which other assessments can be made.

The next requirement that we have as assessors is to determine what kind of 'trainer' we are looking at, or need to recognize. Is he/she an on the job instructor or a direct instructor, a specific instructions type of trainer or one with a more facilitative brief? There is little value in our assessing an instructor type of trainer if what we are looking for are the skills of a facilitator.

A trainer can be expected to fulfil one or more roles within the training organization and the company. Do we expect him to take on the role of the missionary who is trying to make changes through the training role, or are we seeking an educationalist who will deliver 'training' in the procedures, systems and methods in existence in terms of 'this is what you need to know'. Does the trainer need to be so flexible in technique and attitude that he can one day behave in the controlled role of the 'instructor' and the next day in the much more free-ranging role of the human relations facilitator? Again, we must be very clear about the role or roles we are expecting to identify before we set off on the assessment trail.

Company needs

Finally in the general appreciation of the task ahead of us, the demands and requirements of the company itself must be taken into account when we are performing the assessment. What role does the company expect the trainer to fulfil? We may assess a trainer who exhibits all the skills of a highly advance facilitator, group adviser and group/individual therapist, but all the company requires is a 'lecturer' who will *tell* the trainees what they have to know and do! And of course, vice versa. How the trainer meets the company's needs would certainly influence our attitude to the trainer under assessment.

The trainer must adopt a similar initial self-assessment for the same reasons. 'Am I performing the role, not only efficiently and effectively as a trainer, but the one which is required of me by the type of training and the company which I represent?' In many of the trainer assessment events I have run, when this situation has been analysed by the participants, many are faced with the further question 'The answer is "no", so what am I going to/have to do about it?'. The decision must be made, because if a trainer is carrying out roles and tasks which are completely alien to his preferences, attitude and even skill range, he will be frustrated and eventually there will be a reduction in efficiency and effectiveness. Correction through self-assessment (even if the 'remedy' is to leave the situation to find a training job which is more compatible) is vastly preferable to having the deficiencies pointed out by an external assessor. Unfortunately not everybody can take a sufficiently detached point of view to achieve a realistic self-assessment.

Supportive evidence

The training organization may have spent much valuable time on validation analyses of the training, as we saw in the previous two chapters. We saw that information about the skill of the trainer can be gleaned indirectly from these instruments. There must always be some circumspection in using these analyses, however, because of all the possible inconsistencies which can be found, particularly in the inventories on subjects other than knowledge or practical learning. We would be foolish to ignore such possibly supporting evidence for any other approaches we might take, and a planned programme of examining the analyses is an essential part of any assessment programme. If such a training validation programme, not only the end-of-course approach, is not installed in the organization, and trainer assessment is to be performed, introduction of an effective system will greatly aid the trainer assessment programme. Finally, if the *training* validation analyses show a satisfactory position, this may not indicate that the *trainer* is the effective item. Nor, if the training analyses suggest little or reduced learning, do such analyses necessarily mean that the trainer is not doing an effective job.

What are we assessing?

When the matter of *training* assessment was introduced, we saw that the basic element in the process was the need to identify the objectives of the training: what the training was setting out to do, and what the trainees/learners would be expected to know/show/do by the end of the training. At the end of the training, 'tests' of whatever nature were administered to check to what extent these objectives had been achieved.

When we are setting out to assess the trainer, a similar approach is necessary. The trainer's objectives must be assessed as well as those of the training. Under normal circumstances these should be the same, that is, the effective training of or achievement of learning by the people attending the training event or programme. This would appear to be self-evident, but there is always a danger that the objectives of the trainer may not coincide with these aims. The trainer's personal objectives may be much more self-orientated and consciously or subconsciously the trainer may be using the training to satisfy these personal needs. The identification of personal objectives must be, and are, very difficult to achieve by an external assessor; very close attention must be paid to what the trainer says and does to seek clues to the 'hidden agenda'. Usually, in such cases, indications eventually emerge. The most common problem arises when the trainer is being forced to carry out a role which is in strong conflict with his training role preference, and for some reason he is unable to come to terms with the demands of the role. A fairly common example of this might be when the trainer has to carry out training events which carry a particular message from the organization to which the trainer is not committed. In such cases there is the danger that the trainer, overtly or covertly, will try to colour the training with his, rather than the organization's, views.

Trainer needs assessment

Linking the objectives of the trainer and the training/trainees, is the identification of needs. We have seen that meaningful training starts with a complete and accurate identification of the training population's training needs and whether the training suggested fits in with these needs. Similarly with the trainer. What are his needs?

In Chapter Three the range of general skills of a trainer were considered. These were quite sufficient to identify the general role and skill/knowledge/attitude needs of the trainer, but in assessment much more specific information about the presence and absence of these factors is required. A number of approaches to obtaining this information are available ranging from the relatively simple task description to the more comprehensive, holistic description of the competences required by a trainer.

Trainer task analysis

The first example of trainer task analysis is a relatively simple one to complete and can be used as a self-assessment instrument or as an assessment guide by an external assessor. The full instrument is as follows.

AN INVENTORY OF TRAINER SKILLS

The purpose of this inventory is to help you to assess your skills (or assess the skills of another) in a number of training aspects. The emphasis is on the presentation of training sessions, which is the more common activity of many trainers, but the list can obviously be extended to include other types of activity. The results will give you some good indications of your strengths and weaknesses in your training role, and the latter will indicate the areas in which you will have to take developmental action. The inventory will only be of use if you complete it honestly and realistically – complete it as you know the situation *is* rather than how you would like it to be.

Go through the inventory twice. The first time, mark each item in accordance with how you see the present situation. Then go over the list again and identify the priority items which are indicated as your having to take some action. Take the necessary action on these then return to the list to take any necessary further action.

		No problem or not relevant	Satisfactory	Should improve	Must improve
1.	Listening actively	–	–	–	–
2.	Expressing myself clearly	–	–	–	–

3.	Being brief and concise	–	–	–	–
4.	Taking up views expressed	–	–	–	–
5.	Using relevant humour	–	–	–	–
6.	Using real life anecdotes	–	–	–	–
7.	Avoiding jargon	–	–	–	–
8.	Fitting my language to the learner	–	–	–	–
9.	Using my voice efficiently	–	–	–	–
10.	Helping learners understand the difficult points	–	–	–	–
11.	Not forcing my own views in discussion	–	–	–	–
12.	Asking open questions	–	–	–	–
13.	Answering questions effectively	–	–	–	–
14.	Using appropriate non-verbals and gestures	–	–	–	–
15.	Idientifying the learners' learning preference styles	–	–	–	–
16.	Using relevant visual aids	–	–	–	–
17.	Using clear and readable VAs	–	–	–	–
18.	Using clear, readable writing on posters	–	–	–	–
19.	Adding *all* comments by learners to posters	–	–	–	–
20.	Using videos when relevant	–	–	–	–
21.	Using videos effectively	–	–	–	–
22.	Always following up videos with some action	–	–	–	–
23.	Use of other visual aids	–	–	–	–
24.	Able to use range of techniques & methods	–	–	–	–
25.	Being aware of group's behaviour		–	–	–
26.	Being aware of own behaviour	–	–	–	–
27.	Giving instructions effectively	–	–	–	–
28.	Being enthusiastic	–	–	–	–
29.	Coping with conflict within the group	–	–	–	–
30.	Coping with conflict between me and group	–	–	–	–

31.	Handling difficult participants	–	–	–	–
32.	Handling too-high contributing participants	–	–	–	–
33.	Handling too quiet participants	–	–	–	–
34.	Knowing how to 'mix' groups effectively	–	–	–	–
35.	Holding the interest of a group	–	–	–	–
36.	Setting up activities effectively	–	–	–	–
37.	Taking feedback/reportback after activities	–	–	–	–
38.	Commening appropriately after case study interviews	–	–	–	–
39.	Being able to introduce spontaneous input sessions	–	–	–	–
40.	Being able radically to modify programme during the event to satisfy the needs of the learners	–	–	–	–
41.	Other training activities not included in above	–	–	–	–

Completion of this inventory is not an exacting task, but can provide considerable information on which to base developmental consideration and prepare assessors and self-assessors for more comprehensive inventories.

Trainer task inventory

The most useful and commonly used comprehensive inventory relating to the tasks of trainers is the 'Trainer Task Inventory'. This is based on original work in the Air Transport and Travel Industry Training Board by Terry Morgan and Martin Costello. When the Board became defunct, the work was at field trial stage and the British Training Agency (then the Manpower Services Commission) funded Morgan and Costello to complete the work. As a result of further cooperation between the Manpower Services Commission and the Institute for Training and Development the inventory was completed and published in June 1984.

The 'Trainer Task Inventory', or TTI, is essentially a structured task analysis consisting of as full a list as possible of all the tasks carried out by 'trainers'. The tasks are organized into family groups of related tasks, but not necessarily with a particular job holder's role. The flexibility within the TTI enables it to be applied to a variety of trainer roles, with suitable additions and omissions to make the inventory relevant to each. The TTI can be completed by the job holders themselves or by their manager on an assessment/identification basis.

Uses of the TTI

Because of the comprehensive nature of the TTI a number of applications have been suggested for it, in addition to the assessment of the tasks of a training job holder.

Planning
it can help in career choice for people who may be considering entering the profession and want to have some idea of the range of work that would be involved.

Recruitment
This follows from the planning function in that if potential employees are to be encouraged to come to an organization, the more useful information they are given the better for both the recruiter and the applicant. It is inherent, *or should be*, in any recruitment exercise that a job and task analysis should be performed to enable a job profile to be established. From this a preferred person profile is produced to enable the recruiters to compare the candidates with the job requirements.

Organization
The inventory has a use in considering the format of, say, the training department, to determine the structuring of the individual jobs and the overall role requirements of that department. This is particularly useful when a new department has to be set up, although it is equally valuable when an existing department has to be assessed or inspected for validity.

Self-assessment
Because the inventory is sufficiently comprehensive to describe what a trainer should be able to do, an honest self-assessment approach can be achieved to help the job holder to decide what steps are necessary in his self-development

Appraisal
The self-assessment and development approach can be linked readily with the annual appraisal system. One of the common failures of

appraisal systems is that the appraiser has nothing against which to assess the capabilities and competence of the person under appraisal. The TTI at least can help in the identification of what should be within the job holder's repertoire, which leaves the appraiser to assess the level to which these are being achieved.

Role descriptions

The TTI is an extensive instrument which requires time and resource in the initial completion stages, both on the part of the trainers and their managers, but once completed there can be a set of documents which describe all the job processes in the department. As roles and jobs change, and they do, it is relatively simple to ensure that the TTIs are kept up to date with slight amendments rather than repeat full-scale analyses.

Discipline

Although not the intention of the originators of the TTI, and hopefully it may never need to be used for such purposes, it *can* be used in the discipline process. If the need for discipline has arisen as the result of work failings, a probation period is usually set during which the 'offender' is required to improve. The TTI can help to identify areas in which there should be competence and point to those which will be looked at closely during the probation period.

The TTI and assessment

The main use of TTI is in the assessment of the skills and skill range of trainers. It provides at the very minimum a listing of the task areas which a trainer should be capable of doing, which can be moulded to relate directly to whatever trainer role is required. As will be seen later, the level of use of the TTI is itself very flexible, ranging from a simple can/can't do approach, to a more sophisticated one which considers other competence levels.

The structure of the TTI

The basis of the TTI is the fact that there are three major levels of activity in a trainer's task, plus a fourth one concerned with a variety of general principles.

The three levels of activity are:

- Helping people to learn and develop;

124

- Helping people to solve performance problems;
- Helping people to anticipate needs and problems and to formulate policies

Emphasis is on the trainer's role in helping the learners with whom he comes into contact. As we have seen throughout this book there must also be full awareness of the organization's needs. The naive, but realistic answer to this is that the needs of the organization are reflected in the needs of the individual, otherwise the individual does not have a place in the organization. This may appear to be a harsh observation, but previous consideration has shown that if the two needs are not in balance, the training of the learners will be the aspect which will suffer and hence the learners (and consequently the organization) will be the losers.

Helping people to learn and develop includes identifying learning and training needs; designing and preparing for the training events of whatever nature; instructing/training either face to face with individuals or groups, or at a distance with other methods; and evaluating the training provided.

Helping people to solve performance problems involves taking the necessary action to identify performance problems amongst the target population; selecting and designing appropriate intervening strategies; implementing the intervention; and evaluating the results of the interventions. In the TTI parlance an 'intervention' is 'any activity undertaken to overcome an identified problem.'

Helping people to anticipate needs and problems and to formulate policies relates to the identification of future needs and problems; and the formulation of strategies and plans to deal with these.

The final activity was labelled *General Functions* and included all factors which would support some or all the other activities – administration, management, knowing the organization and self-development.

When compared with the skills of an effective trainer as considered earlier in this book, a number of factors appear to be missing. One of the main advantages of the TTI is its flexibility so that omissions, *which are necessary elements of a particular trainer's job,* can always be added. One criticism which can be levelled at the TTI is the absence of guidance on the personal behavioural aspects required in the job – effectiveness does not necessarily imply completely appropriate behaviour. As subsequent competence assessors have discovered this is the 'black hole' of assessment and one which causes most discussion. At least the TTI addresses the factual task of the job in a realistic and usable way.

The structure of the TTI is progressive – whether you look at the progression from the bottom to the top or top to bottom is not too relevant. The TTI takes the latter course and describes:

- The four Levels of Activity briefly described above;
- A number of Work Areas within each Level of Activity;
- A number of Task Groups (or tasks) within each Work Area.

The TTI contains four Levels of Activity, 17 Work Areas distributed unevenly throughout the levels, and 252 tasks, with spaces for additional task entries. A description of the evolution of the inventory and the method of using it precedes 21 A4 pages of Levels, Areas and Tasks. It is not possible to include here the complete document, copies of which can be obtained from the Institute of Training and Development, but the following will give the flavour of the format.

TTI format

The first Level of Activity which is concerned with 'Helping people to learn and develop' is subdivided into seven Work Areas, each Work Area having from 4 to 23 Task Groups.

As an example, Work Area 4 is concerned with *Preparing for training/learning events* and contains the following 23 Task Groups.

1. Write/update manuals
2. Write programmed texts
3. Write handouts
4. Design visual aids – viewfoils, etc.
5. Make visual aids – viewfoils, etc.
6. Design audio-visual aids (videos/films)
7. Make audio-visual aids (videos/films)
8. Set up and position audio-visual equipment
9. Repair damaged equipment
10. Purchase training material
11. Negotiate resources/training facilities in hotels
12. Choose outside speakers
13. Brief outside speakers
14. Carry out pre-course interviews with trainees
15. Send out joining instructions
16. Analyse pre-course reports on trainees by their managers
17. Test out alternative methods/media
18. Write case studies
19. Investigate ready-made courses/materials
20. Design trainee self-assessment instruments
21. Develop computer-managed instructional material
22. Prepare tape/slide script material
23. Design tape/slide visual material
24. ——
25. ——
26. ——
27. ——
28. ——
29. ——
30. ——

126

It will be immediately apparent that a number of these tasks are not relevant to *some* trainers, whereas other trainers will say immediately that there are a number of omissions when they consider their own job. This is so; the former need only debate those items which are not relevant to them, and the latter add the tasks which relate to them and which are not shown in the spaces provided. Consequently, when an individual TTI is completed, there should be considerably more than the original 252 tasks or considerably fewer. For example, when I was employed in one organization as a direct, management training trainer, I was not concerned at all in tasks 2, 9, 11, 12, 13, 15 and 21, although there were at least eight other tasks which I could have added to the list. This is the way the TTI is intended to be used, it is not a definitive document.

Using the TTI

The flexibility of the TTI is not restricted to the Task Group entries, but there are a number of ways which it can be used in practice. The start of an actual page (in fact the one from which the Task Groups listed above were taken) is in the following format and you will notice that it contains one method of using the inventory.

Work Area 4: Preparing for training/learning events.	1	2	3	4
Listed below is a task group and the tasks it includes. Tick against all tasks which you perform. Add at the bottom any tasks you do which are not listed.				
Task Group	if done			

1. Write/update manuals
etc.

In the example shown, the trainer is invited to place a tick in column 1 against all the tasks performed and to add any which are not shown. Obviously if one of the tasks is not performed, no tick is placed in column 1. The immediate question raised by this omission is 'Is this part of the job which *should* be performed and therefore action has to be taken to allow it to be ticked?' This is an immediate assessment, not necessarily of the trainer's competence, but one which identifies what he should be doing. The remaining columns offer options to the use of the TTI.

One approach which I have used and have found particularly useful is to use the TTI not only as an identification of tasks which should be performed, but also an identification of the level of competence attained (or at least a subjective assessment of this). Instead of four columns, I use only one, although there are variations which can use more than the one column. Delete all the tasks which are definitely not relevant and add those which have not been included.

When this has been done, work through all the entries and against each entry mark either a tick, a cross, an asterisk, a zero or any other preferred mark. If the competence level is non-existent, mark no entry. If that aspect is known, but at a superficial level only, place one mark; if it is known or is at a skill level above the superficial level, but not to such an extent that the person would be capable of performing it effectively, place two marks; if they could perform it effectively or satisfactorily, place three marks; if there is complete competence, four marks. A look down the one column will then immediately show where strengths and weaknesses, competences and training needs lie. If columns are retained, each column can be used for a different level of competence and the 'dog-leg' picture which emerges will show strengths and weaknesses clearly.

The published TTI describes other uses which have been introduced by some organizations. The United States Air Force, from whose original work the TTI developed, uses column one as shown, that is that the task has been completed. Column two is devoted to *time spent* on the task and a grading of 1 to 7 is used here. Column three also has a 7 point coded scale concerned with *importance*.

Other options used have been :

1.
Column 1 (if used)   is marked if the task has been performed in the past 18 months.
Column 2   is marked if the task has been carried out in the past 18 months but the trainer feels it should not be tackled by them
Column 3   is marked if the task has *not* been carried out in the past 18 months but the trainer feels it should be tackled by them
Column 4   is marked if the trainer feels they need further training or guidance.

2.
Column 1 (if used)   is marked if the task is completed.
Column 2   is marked if the task is not being tackled, but should be part of the job
Column 3   is marked if the task is being tackled but should not be part of the job.

These four examples demonstrate the flexibility of the TTI and the fact that it can be used in a variety of ways, many depending on your own needs.

The TTI can itself be used as a simple checklist when a trainer is self-assessing or a trainer is being assessed by an external assessor. Either use demands that a basic document showing the full extent (and constraints) of the job should have been completed and agreed upon – this defines the job against which any assessment can be made. It must be appreciated, however, that the TTI is used to assess tasks and their performance, more than a means of assessing the competence level within a particular task or operation, but it gives the assessor an inventory of *what* can then be assessed for competence.

Competence standards

The TTI, although a valuable and useful inventory, and one which has served and is still serving its purpose well, is in many ways a crude device. Several years ago the British government made a statement of intention that there would be national standards developed for all occupations by 1991. The purpose of these standards was to give assessors in a variety of areas real tools on which too measure the competences of working people at all levels. The standards would certainly be part of a movement to increase the professional, occupational, and above all, educational qualifications of people in industry and commerce. Consequently, with the support of the Training Agency, bodies such as the Management Charter Initiative and the National Council for Vocational Qualifications led the way for standards to be produced.

One of the first of these which has established the format for subsequent standards was the 'Management Competences Standards Project' (MCS). The purpose of this was to define, holistically, the competences required by managers of whatever nature. The holistic approach to this definition has set it further along the trail than many of the task analyses which preceded it. The MCS is generic for managers and is applicable whether the management role is in engineering, commerce, pharmaceuticals or farming.

The basis of the MCS is known as functional analysis which looks at the whole job rather than concentrating on the tasks. The first definition in the analysis is that competence is defined as 'the ability to perform activities within an occupation to the standards expected'.

Following this definition comes the identification of a manager's role in progressively detailed terms.

The key purpose

The start of the description is the Key Purpose, which, in terms of the manager's role, is 'to achieve the organization's objectives and continuously improve its performance'. Wherever a manager may be located, and whatever the specific role might be, this purpose must be at the heart of every manager's job. However important this statement might be, it must be made more specific in order that assessment of the standards might be possible.

The key role

The next level of a manager's job is determined by what are described as the Key Roles. These are the discrete areas of responsibility, and for a 'generic' manager have been defined as:

- Managing operations,
- Managing finance,
- Managing people,
- Managing information, and
- Personal competences.

These Key Roles are the forces by which the Key Purpose is achieved, and describe how it will be achieved, but still not with sufficient detail to enable assessment.

Units

Units are the basic building bricks of the functional analysis on which the standards are universally determined and follow on naturally from the Key Roles.

Each Key Role will contain a number of Units, the actual number varying from one Key Role to another, depending on its complexity. For example, the Key Role relating to the financial responsibilities of a manager contains two Units, which are:

- Monitor and control the use of resources;
- Secure effective resource allocation for activities and projects.

Other Roles break down into different numbers of Units, e.g. Managing People has four Units.

Elements

The statements of Roles and Units describe 'what' a manager does, rather than the 'how'. This more detailed description is left to the Elements into which each Unit is divided. For example, two Elements are involved in the Unit concerned with monitoring and controlling the use of resources (each Unit will contain a number of Elements, again depending on the complexity of the work). The Elements in our example Unit are:

- Control costs and enhance value;
- Monitor and control activities against budgets

Performance criteria

The next step is to detail the ways in which the success of these objectives or the competence of the manager can be examined and assessed. Other factors will obviously be necessary for a full assessment, but a set of Performance Criteria will take the assessment a considerable distance. Once again, the preceding levels are divided into a number of parts, the number depending on the complexity of the work. If we take the Element which requires the manager to monitor and control activities against budget, the Performance Criteria to check the competence of these include:

- Expenditure is within agreed limits, does not compromise future spending requirements and conforms to the organization's policy and procedures;
- Requests for expenditure outside the manager's responsibility are referred promptly to the appropriate people;
- Where appropriate, expenditure is phased in accordance with a planned time scale;

and so on to a total of eight criteria.

Range indicators

The final detail which must be considered relates to the variations which can occur within an occupation. If all these were to be included in the main body of the statement, it would become too extensive and too detailed to be a usable document. Instead, in any set of standards, the basic generic elements are shown, but all the possible variations are included under the title of 'Range Indicators' (originally called 'Range Statements').

Using our Element example of 'Monitor and control activities against budgets', the relevant Range Indicators include:

- Monitoring relates to an accounting centre for which the manager has responsibility;
- Monitoring covers
  a) direct costs of
     materials
     staffing
     expenses
  b) relevant overhead charges
  c) any revenue earned by the accounting centre
  d) cash flow;
- Expenditure outside the manager's area of responsibility will be due to it;
  a) being over stated budget limits
  b) subject to other organizational controls,

and so on.

The draft statement current in mid-1990 of Key Purpose, Key Roles, Units and Elements for the occupation standards for managers (middle managers II) is shown in Figure 10.1.

The set of Performance Criteria and Range Indicators for one of the Elements is shown in Figure 10.2.

Trainer standards

As mentioned earlier, the range of occupations is being considered for the production of standards which can be applied across industries and sectors. These are being developed by what are described as Lead Bodies, and the format of the standards statements being produced follows generally that described for the generic manager. Some, particularly those of the less complex occupations, may concentrate on Units, Elements and Performance Criteria, the building bricks of competence

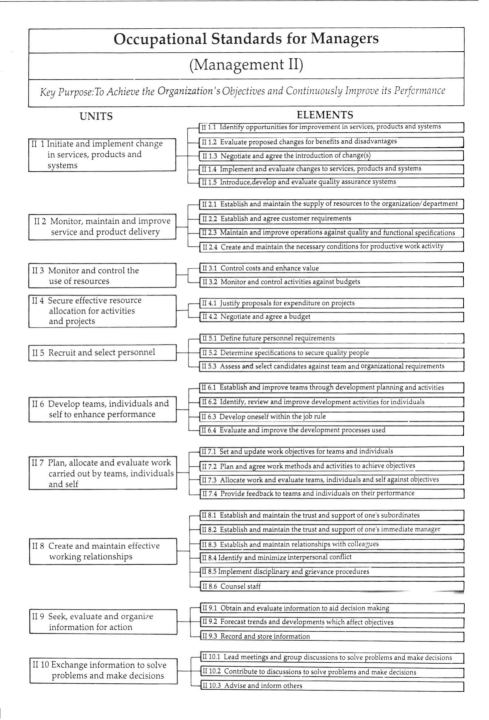

Figure 10.1

(Reproduced with permission of the Department of Employment's Training, Education and Enterprise Division)

Occupational Standards for Managers
(Management II)
Key Purpose: To Achieve the Organization's Objectives and Continuously Improve its Performance

Key Role Manage Finance

Unit II 3 Monitor and control the use of resources

Element II 3.2 Monitor and control activities against budgets

Performance Criteria:

(a) Expenditure is within agreed limits, does not compromize future spending requirements and conforms to the organization's policy and procedures

(b) Requests for expenditure outside the manager's responsibility are referred promptly to the appropriate people

(c) Where appropriate, expenditure is phased in accordance with a planned time scale

(d) Actual income and expenditure is checked against agreed budgets at regular, appropriate intervals

(e) Where a budget shortfall is likely to occur, the appropriate people are informed with minimum delay

(f) Any necessary authority for changes in allocation between budget heads is obtained in advance of requirement

(g) Any modifications to agreed budgets during the accounting period are consistant with agreed guidelines and correctly authorized

(h) Prompt, corrective action is taken where necessary in response to significant deviations from budget

Range indicators:

Monitoring relates to an accounting centre for which the manager has responsibility.

Monitoring covers:
- direct costs of:
    materials
    staffing
    expenses
- relevant overhead charges
- any revenue earned by the accounting centre
- cash flow.

Expenditure outside the manager's area of responsibility will be due to it:
- being over stated budget limits
- subject to other organizational controls.

The manager authorizes expenditure in accordance with the organization's financial procedures.

Corrective action includes:
- advising subordinates to alter/ modify their activities
- altering budget allocations within the limits of responsibility
- rescheduling expenditure.

Figure 10.2

(Reproduced with permission of the Department of Employment's Training, Education and Enterprise Division)

standards based on functional analysis. All standards statements will then fulfil the purpose of enabling assessors to satisfy themselves that people are performing their occupations to the competence levels required.

Training and development is an area which crosses industry and sector boundaries and has been one of the subjects for development of competence standards; it clearly has an important bearing on the question of assessment of the trainer. Not only can the trainer be assessed, but this may be in the knowledge that this assessment is being applied against a nationally agreed level and set of criteria. It may be applied not only for internal assessment purposes, but can also be used to support the achievement of professional, vocational qualifications which can be used not only across the profession, but in transfer to other areas of work.

The body responsible for establishing this framework is the Training and Development Lead Body and the results published in January 1991 are intended to cover a range of training and development practitioners from trainers to training consultants, and human resource managers.

The standards framework proposed by the TDLB are shown in Figure 10.3. Performance Criteria and Range Statements follow this framework. At this stage it gives a good indication of the range of functions available for assessment which are followed by a trainer.

Qualifications which the TDLB aim to measure using the standards, those awarded by NCVQ, ScotVec, BTEC, City and Guilds, etc., will be at the higher assessment levels (3, 4 and 5). Level 3 will offer statements of competence for, training officers or trainers who deliver training specified and designed by others, assess the outcomes of that training and design training from given directives. Level 4 is that of the training manager who may also be involved in training and who identifies, designs, delivers and evaluates at the corporate and management level. Level 5 is the Human Resource Development manager at the strategic design and delivery of training systems level.

Many bodies interested in training and development have been involved in this development, including the bodies currently offering qualifications – ITD, IPM, etc. The ultimate VQs must reflect the quality previously maintained by these bodies, and those supported at a higher level by postgraduate work, e.g. M.Phil (Training and Development), M.Ed (Training and Development), among others. At the very least the standards will give organizations a measure by which to assess the trainers in their employ and the VQs will give a qualification to training and development staff which will be nationally recognized at identifiable levels of competence.

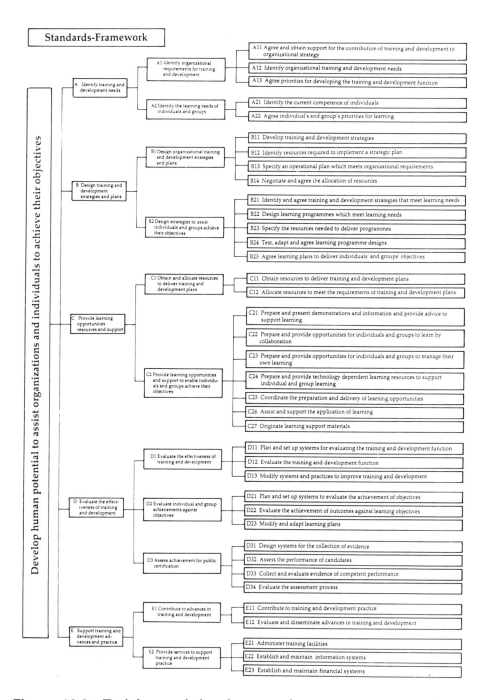

Figure 10.3 Training and development key purpose, areas, key roles and units of performance

Trainer standards key roles, units and elements

The key purpose of training and development defined by the TDLB is 'Develop human potential to assist organizations and individuals to achieve their objectives'. Within this five key areas in training and development have been identified by the TDLB:

A Identify training and development needs;
B Design training and development strategies and plans;
C Provide learning opportunities resources and support;
D Evaluate the effectiveness of training and development;
E Support training and development advances and practice.

Each key area or principal function is sub-divided into either two or three key roles identified by the codes A1, A2; B1, B2, etc. For example, key role A1 is 'Identify organizational requirements for training and development'; A2 is 'Identify the learning needs of individuals and groups'. Figure 10.3 summarizes all the key roles contained in the standards.

Training and development standards are broken down into more detailed elements in the same way that the generic manager standards were subdivided from the key role level.

Key role A1 has three Units of Performance;
All Agree and obtain support for the contribution of training and development in organizational strategy;
A12 Identify organizational training and development needs;
A13 Agree priorities for developing the training and development function.

Other key roles have similarly associated units of performance and these are given in Figure 10.3. If we follow key role A1 through the standards we see (Figure 10.4) that each unit A11, A12 and A13 has between two and four Elements of Performance – these are coded A111, A112; A121, A122, A123, A124; A131, A132, A133. It will be seen that unit A11 which is 'Agree and obtain support for the contribution of training and development to organizational strategy' contains two elements, A111 and A112.

A111 states: 'Agree the contribution of training and development to organizational strategy'.

A112 states: 'Promote and support decision makers' commitment to the agreed contribution of training and development'.

Figure 10.5 describes these two elements and the two other aspects of standards – performance Criteria and Range Indicators.

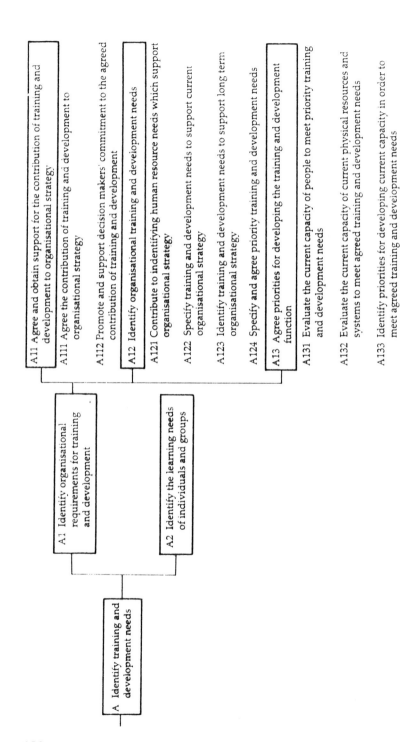

Figure 10.4 Training and development units and elements

A11 AGREE AND OBTAIN SUPPORT FOR THE CONTRIBUTION OF TRAINING AND DEVELOPMENT TO ORGANIZATIONAL STRATEGY   A1

A111 Agree the contribution of training and devlopment to organizational strategy

a Proposals are presented which identify relevant training and development contributions that support organizational strategy

b Where relevant, proposals are based on evaluations of previous contributions of training and development to organizational policy

c Proposals match training and development options to organizational policies

d Options which have the greatest potential for success are recommended and promoted

e Policy makers are given opportunities to ask questions and seek clarification

f Negotiations and agreements are conducted and concluded in a manner which promotes and maintains goodwill and trust

g Agreed options are accurately summarized and made availbale to those who need the information

Range indicators

Organizational stratgegies: proactive/supply led; reactive/demand led

Relationship with policy makers: peer/subordinate/superior: inside/outside own organization: employer/employee/client

Sources of evidence for options: internal/external; research and survey reports/professional and trade press

Training and development options

Presentation methods: oral,written, audio-visual, computer-based

Presentation/negotiation processes: direct/face to face; remote/via systems (such as teleconferencing systems)

A112 Promote and support decision makers' commitment to the agreed contribution of training and development

a The relationship between training and development's agreed contribution and the priorities of decision makers is accurately identified

b Presentations are made to decision makers which clearly identify and realistically evaluate the agreed contribution of training and development

c Accurate and appropriate analyses of added value and costs and benefits of training and development are made available to decision makers

d Non-tangible benefits are identified, accurately and realistically evaluated and promoted to decision makers

e Relevant examples of positive organizational outcomes from training and development are identified and made availbale to decision makers

f Decision makers are given opportunities to ask questions and seek clarification

g The information and support required by decision makers in order for them to promote training and development is sought from them, agreed and provided

Range indicators

Sources for priorities: business plans/reports; performance reports (formal/informal); anecdotal data; formal/informal data collection

Relationship with decision makers : peer/ subordinate/superior: inside/outside own organization: employer/employee/client:

Organizational benefits: quantative/qualitative: organizational mission: competitive advantage:

Management of skill supply: impact on local/national/international economy: impact on local/national/international community

Sources of evidence and examples: research: organizational reports and records:networks:professional organizations/journals

Presentation methods:oral,written,audio-visual,computer-based

Presentation/dissemination processes: direct/face to face: indirect (such as reports, discussion papers/newletters): remote/via systems (such as teleconferencing systems)

Types of support to decision makers: information: materials: equipment: facilities: administrative/professional services

Figure 10.5 Training and development elements, performance criteria and range indicators

(Figures 10.3, 10.4, 10.5 and 10.6 are reproduced here with the permission of the Employment Department, TEED, from the TDLB National Standards for Training and Development' [Employment Department, January 1991, price £10]).

The Performance Criteria are the practical aids to assessing competence in training and development. In effect, they are the questions from which it can be decided through the responses given, whether the individual being asked either can or can't do the function involved. The number of criteria will obviously reflect the complexity of the element of performance. Both elements A111 and A112 for example have seven performance criteria each. Other elements have more, others less. For example, element C272 has ten performance criteria, D221 has four, etc.

In addition to the performance criteria, each element has a number of Range Indicators (also shown in Figure 10.5). The range indicators can be used to vary the standards and define the range of applications of the element, that is the types of relationships, resources, methods, processes and locations, for which achievement of the specified outcomes is required. In this way the criticism can be avoided that the standards are too narrow and do not cover every situation variation. If all possibilities were to be included in one standard statement, although this would be comprehensive, it would also be so extensive and detailed that it would be too unwieldy to use. Introducing the range indicators, the standards can be added to or subtracted from to cover any training and development situation.

Practical applications

Whichever turns out to be the most effective – the Trainer Task Inventory described earlier, or the Competence Standards – one painful fact will have become apparent. There is no approach which does not involve a complex and perhaps exceptionally long listing of factors to be taken into account. This is particularly so when we consider a varied type of occupation such as that of a trainer – of whatever ilk – and an assessment is made of the degree of complexity. If the tasks and roles are simplified to too great an extent, there may be little value in the end result. If the list of items to be assessed is too long, the instrument may not be used because of the inherent difficulties. Compromises would seem to be available, but in this field this may be more ineffective than the extremes.

Much may depend on the way the inventory is to be used. If it is to be simply a catalogue of tasks which, once completed, requires only occasional updating and modification, an extensive listing may be acceptable. However, if a working instrument with constant reference is necessary a different format of guidelines must be introduced. What is encouraging is that notice is now being taken of analyses which, with assessment, can be utilized in many ways – recruitment, appraisal, selection, assessment for job and qualification, job description, and so on. Although the task may appear monumental, once produced, and provided the will to maintain it is there, a long lasting instrument will be available.

11

Trainer assessment in action

All the ingredients for the assessment of a trainer have now been described with the exception of the two final factors:

- Assessment planning
- Assessment instrumentation

Both of these play an important part in the effective assessment of the trainer and will be dealt with here.

The recipe for a full assessment of the trainer's effectiveness is the utilization of many instruments, inventories, occasions and methods. It is not sufficient to use only one of these, otherwise the assessment is unlikely to be complete and therefore less effective than it might be. Care has to be taken lest the number and complexity of the instruments might take over from the prime task of actually assessing the trainer. The task cannot be approached in a haphazard manner, however, or with the attitude 'Oh, I'll be able to cope without any of those bits of paper!'.

You must first decide what you are going to look for and with which resources. A first principle must be that you will be looking for the best practices known and accepted, bearing in mind the role(s) expected of the trainer and the role(s) required by the organization.

What are you going to use in your assessment? A trainer is likely to be involved in one or more of input sessions; discussions; activities, games and exercises; role play enactments; case studies; open learning support; visual aid design and/or production; and so on. Which of these are to be included in the assessment? Some or all?

How often is the assessment to be made? How often are the different features of the trainer's job to be observed or assessed in some other way? Which type of inventory or listing of tasks is to be used?

The questions above are but a few of those which the assessor will need to address before an assessment is commenced. There must be an assessment plan to satisfy the circumstances in which the assessment is to be made.

Who?

The first question must be 'Who is going to perform the assessment?' This decision will obviously depend on the size of the training organization, the size and culture of the organization itself and the resources available.

In an organization with a large training department with a number of trainers, compared with the 'one-man' type of training department, two principal options are available. One must be that the Training Manager or other management level person directly responsible for trainers will be the natural assessor – this will relate directly to any annual appraisal system in operation, Or, if, as so often happens, the person responsible for the trainers is not a trainer but perhaps the Personnel Manager or Director, a different approach may be necessary. These non-trainers may not have the resources, time or expertise to assess professional trainers. Their recourse would be to external agencies who have expertise in the training and assessment of trainers.

A compromise situation, in which I was involved as an external consultant, resulted in the identification within the organization of several people of responsible level, with an interest in training, who were then themselves trained to be assessors with sufficient knowledge of the skills and techniques of training, not to make *them* training experts, but to enable them to know when training was being performed effectively.

Two criteria are involved here. The assessor must be a responsible person who has an obvious link with the person to be assessed. When the external assessor is introduced problems can be created when their assessment is challenged on a knowledge of the industry/company or other credibility factors. The training knowledge skill of the external assessor is assumed, otherwise they would/should not have been appointed, but the internal assessor runs the danger of being accused of not being a trainer/not knowing what training is really all about and so on. It should be demonstrable in the former case that the external assessor has the credibility and in the latter case, the assessor should not be allowed to be in the assessment position without the necessary knowledge.

Who else?

One of the problems of assessing such a subjective event as the effectiveness of the activities of a trainer is that the assessment by the assessor, however skilled and experienced he might be, will almost certainly be clouded in some way by value judgements. Everybody has views on a variety of subjects, consciously or subconsciously, and even with awareness of these and their dangers, it is difficult to assess subjective happenings without involving their values. A typical example in the case of assessing trainers is that the assessor must have an extensive knowledge of training, its methods, techniques and approaches. Some suggest that in order to assess another trainer, the assessor must himself have the skills of an effective trainer. Others suggest that personal skills are not necessary in the assessor, but he must possess a very wide knowledge of the techniques, methods and approaches in training; be up to date with advances in training methods and technology; and have the skill to advise the trainer who knows that the assessor is not himself a skilled trainer.

The assumption made in many cases is that the best assessors are the ones who probably have been successful trainers themselves and can therefore appreciate more readily what the trainer is trying to do. This is a strong argument, but I do not necessarily believe that it is the most effective answer. Certainly he must have a very extensive knowledge, but if he is or has been a trainer there is always the danger that he will bring with him, albeit subconsciously, his own value judgements based on his own training activities. The views may be right or wrong, but the problem is that, as the trainer to be assessed is being observed to train in a particular way, the assessor may think that the approach used may not be the best/most appropriate one because (subconsciously) 'I used to do that in a different, i.e. better way, therefore he isn't being as effective as he could be'.

One method of reducing this danger is for there to be at least two assessors in the hope that their two sets of value judgements will cancel each other out! Or one will observe what the other has missed, or the two balanced views will strengthen the assessment. The luxury of at least two assessors is not always available however, so the views of one assessor must be considered with a modicum of reserve.

The question which follows this is often 'Who assesses the assessors?', a very relevant question to pose. In many cases, if all the assessment is performed by internally based assessors, assessment of the assessors, or sometimes a checking assessment of a sample of trainers is undertaken by an external, neutral assessor.

If the assessor, as suggested above, is a non-trainer, he should have knowledge of training and development skills, techniques, methods, approaches and advances as extensive as possible. If, as is not uncommon in the case of organizations initiating an assessment programme of this nature, a number of assessors have been appointed to carry out the trainer assessment programme, the organization should ensure that they are all:

- As knowledgeable as each other to the extent suggested above;
- Able to assess trainers in a consistent manner.

What usually happens is that a workshop is held to train these assessors in:

- Assessment techniques;
- Training knowledge.

In this way the assessors with no or little knowledge and personal skills are brought to the same standard of knowledge as those with some previous experience as a trainer. The training in this case differs somewhat from that given to trainers, but in many ways is very similar.

Self-assessment

It may be that a trainer has no line manager who is willing or able to assess him, or the Training Manager may be the same person as the trainer. In such a situation the effective option is for self-assessment to take place. This will not be as effective as an independent assessment by an external assessor, but is better than nothing if an assessor is not available. As far as possible, the trainer will use the same approaches and instruments that would be used by the assessor, modified as necessary to provide self-assessment.

Most questionnaires or inventories used as aides by an external assessor can be used by the trainer, but the direct observation possible by an assessor is not available. However, it may be possible to videorecord the event so that the trainer can view the recording after the event, and try to assess what he sees, imagining that he is an external assessor performing an assessment on the trainer shown in the video.

Even without the luxuries of CCTV or audio recording, it is possible to self-assess using an assessment questionnaire. Here again complete honesty, as far as self-assessment allows, is required.

Self-assessment need not only be the alternative to no assessment at all. The comment was made earlier about the problem of value judgements of a single assessor – this is even greater in self-assessment, but if an assessment is made of, say, a trainer's presentational session by the assessor, a parallel attempt at assessment can also be made by the trainer.

As far as possible the trainer should attempt self-assessment using the same instruments as the assessor, direct observation being replaced if possible by CCTV recording. After the event, the two assessments can be used in the post-event discussion and any differences explained and justified by the use of real-life examples.

Peer assessment

It is quite common for a training course or other training event to be carried out by more than one trainer. Quite often, when one of the trainers is taking a session, the other(s) are away from the course working on other tasks or preparing for their own sessions. When assessment is taking place, the trainer being assessed could negotiate with one of the other trainers to sit in on the session and perform an assessment in exactly the same way as that being performed by the main assessor. The same instruments and methods would need to be used, so that following the event a consistent comparison could be made during the assessment discussion. In this case three 'assessments' could be involved – that of the 'official' assessor, the self-assessment of the trainer, and the external assessment by the peer trainer. Part of the negotiation with the colleague trainer could be agreement to do the same for him when it is his turn for assessment.

One of the disadvantages of using a peer assessor is not that of the peer constraints, but that one more non-participating person is being introduced into the learner group. This could have the same effect on the learners' attitudes as the injection of the main assessor into their learning community.

Trainee assessment

This approach is perhaps the least successful, and has the highest risk level in assessing the trainer's effectiveness. It should follow very naturally that the best people to assess the trainer are the learners who have been the trainer's audience. They will generally be too involved in the learning process to take too much notice of the skills of the trainer, may complicate an assessment of the trainer with assessment of the training – these could be two completely different things – and in any case may not be aware of the skills necessary and used in the process of helping them to learn.

Having said that, the views of the learners should not be ignored. They are certainly considered when we are trying to assess the value of the training and as we have shown, training assessment may have implications for trainer assessment. One approach, often thought too risky by many trainers and training managers, is to ask the learners to complete a simplified assessment questionnaire based on that used by the assessor(s).

The disadvantage of using the learners centres principally on the question of the level of honesty of people who have been deeply involved in the process and consequently in training relationships. If the trainer has been liked (whether or not the training has been effective) or disliked, these attitudes are very likely to cloud the validity of the assessment – much more than that of an external assessor, and, to some extent, a peer assessor.

Assessments by learners would not be taken in isolation, so could form a useful supplement to the other assessments made. A possible questionnaire format is suggested later when we consider observation instruments.

Where?

This should be the easiest question to answer. Effective assessment cannot usually take place outside the workplace. It can be argued that to some extent assessment of a learner can be made during a training event. Earlier in the book testing was discussed and effective tests were considered. It must be realized that although these might be effective tests, they are only so at the time and in the training situation. The trainee gas meter reader receives his training, is tested and passes the terminal test completely – in the training situation. But real life can present additional challenges. The training event cannot replicate *all* the possible problems the meter reader might, and does, face out in the real world – menacing dogs or other animals, unhygienic conditions, difficult locations, antagonistic householders, and so on. The training lays the basic grounding in a skill, the real reinforcement of this learning and the effective validation is what happens on the front line.

Certainly, non-operational situations can be included in the overall assessment plan, but these must supplement the principal approach. The most effective assessment will occur when the trainer is doing his job – actually training a person or group of people.

Many difficulties can be envisaged in doing this. The presence of a 'third party' in the training room can be unsettling both for the trainer and the learners. The trainer knows why the assessor is there and, unless he is a very experienced and confident person, this presence will have some effect, which will vary, depending on the personality of the trainer, his confidence and the amount of control he has over his behaviour. I have assessed trainers responsible to me on the progress of their careers – I know that on at least one occasion the performance of one of the trainers during the training session was completely different from his normal class behaviour. His normal behaviour existed before my assessment and persisted after the event; the temporary change was for my benefit alone. Fortunately there are other ways that some information can be gained.

The presence of the assessor can also have a disturbing influence on the learners. The honest way would seem to be to tell them why the assessor was there, that he was not assessing them but the trainer. I see many dangers in this. The learners may have formed a bond with the trainer whom they 'like' – irrespective of whether he is a good trainer. In such circumstances there is every danger that they will do all they can to make the trainer shine in the eyes of the assessor. Difficulties which would normally have been raised may be forced to lie dormant; questions or statements to help discussion along might be made when normally they would remain unspoken, and so on. All this may occur without any reference to the trainer and the learners' behaviour might actually detract from the trainer's intended performance. It may be more appropriate to let the group know that the assessor's presence is not unusual; it happens from time to time and is threatening to no-one. Whether the learners believe this depends on the skill of the person explaining the reasons for the assessor's presence!

When?

The actual occasions on which the assessor observes the trainer in action may be critical and certainly may go some way to resolving such problems as those raised in the previous section. If the trainer behaves out of character on one occasion, to impress the assessor, a repeat performance on a second occasion becomes more difficult, and a third occasion is almost certain to show more normal behaviour.

Observation on one occasion only will therefore have a limited benefit and circumstances will dictate how many additional observations are necessary. Time may be the restricting factor in this, but if assessment is to be made effectively, time must be made available. Other factors will also have to be taken into account. If the trainer is 'known' to be effective, the planning will not include extensive observation, but there must be sufficient to ensure that a true assessment is made and the 'known effectiveness' is valid. Under normal circumstances two observations of a particular event may be sufficient in such cases. When the first observation shows that there are shortcoming, after discussion with the trainer followed perhaps by training where this is necessary, further observations to confirm the improvement will be necessary. Again, at least two observations of effective performance will be necessary.

What?

'What' will be assessed through observation or otherwise will obviously depend on the reason for assessment and the nature of the training in which the trainers to be assessed are involved.

Presentational events

A number of organizations which train their employees through an internal training department do so by means of input sessions, presentations or talks. The trainer stands or sits in front of the class and proceeds to give the instruction or talk. Visual aids of various types may or may not be used, but essentially the approach is didactic.

The observations of a trainer who has to perform are fairly simple. Observations will be made while the trainer is presenting his session and account will need to be taken of the two principal factors involved – presentation skills and within these, the use of visual aids.

Advanced presentational events

Presentational events are often developed beyond the stand and 'tell 'em' approach, ranging from simply questioning the group to obtain answers, through the initiation and build up of a discussion on a part of the topic, or the introduction of a game, exercise or role play associated with the subject of the session. If some or all of these are included in the session, the observation must be extended to incorporate these separate, different skills. Discussion has a particular technique: questions can be put in an effective or ineffective manner and the type of question may be governed by the event; games, exercises and role plays, the participants briefed, the activity controlled, trainer intervention occurring whenever necessary, and at the end there will be a feedback period or assessment of the participants' involvement. The different activities require different types of observation. The various training methods described here can also form events or session themselves and will require appropriate observation. A training session may consist of question and answer, or discussion only, or the two approaches may be combined. The assessor must be prepared, and sufficiently skilled, to identify the approaches being used to assess:

- Their relevance to the specific situation;
- Their effectiveness in use.

Other training activities

Similar comments can apply to the assessment of a trainer who might include video presentations, computer programs and practical demonstrations/applications within his training. The assessor must have the necessary skill and instruments with which to measure the effectiveness of the trainer, not only in his use of these technological aids, but in whether the most appropriate aid is being used and whether it is being introduced in the most effective way and at the most appropriate time.

Assessment action prior to the training

Effective practice of training is not exclusively reliant on the direct delivery in front of the learners. If the trainer has been responsible for:

- The identification of the training needs;
- Decision-making on the type of training approach to satisfy the training need;
- The design and construction of the training instrument – open learning package, course, session, video, computer program and so on;
- The design, development and possibly production of visual and audio aids.

Other assessment action will be necessary. Observation of the end product will suggest its effectiveness, but without understanding of the background and more particularly the training terminal objectives, assessment of effectiveness can only be guessed at.

It is necessary therefore to discuss these factors with the trainer before observing the event so that the assessor has a full appreciation of the training. The logical approach is to arrange with the trainer which events the assessor will be observing and determine which of those listed above were in the hands of the trainer, how they were approached and for what reasons, and what was the eventual decision about the objectives set for the training.

A similar discussion must be held as soon after the observed training as possible. During this discussion the assessor will be interested in hearing the views of the trainer about:

- Whether he felt the session was successful or not, and why this was felt;
- Whether he felt that the objectives determined beforehand had been met or not, and why either of these results were achieved;
- Whether all the aids had been used effectively or not;
- Whether all the supporting techniques – videos, etc. – had been used effectively or not, and why;
- Any ways in which the trainer feels the session could be improved.

151

The assessor will have formed his own views on these subjects and a developmental discussion can result from the comparison of the two views, particularly if they are divergent in any way.

How?

The last question to ask about the process of trainer assessment is concerned with the manner, the methods, the 'how' of assessment.
I see this as having three parts:

- Observation of the trainer in action;
- Discussion with the trainer and others, before and after the observation; and
- The use of supplementary evidence – validation and evaluation processes.

Supplementary evidence

Although the end-of-course validation and other training validation and evaluation measures are concerned with training, they must have a place in the assessment of the trainer. The various approaches have been considered in some detail earlier and in particular the end-of-course validation instruments. However, as we saw, too much credence must not be placed on these validation measures because:

- If they are all highly congratulatory there will inevitably be a suspicion of euphoria or too close a relationship with the trainer as a person;
- If they are all more deprecatory, there may be a suspicion that 'I didn't like that trainer' and a consequent downrating of their views. In addition to, or instead of that feeling, they might be saying 'He didn't teach me anything'.

There will be, of course, events which will justify a high scoring throughout and by all the learners, but a more realistic result will show a spread in rating which depends on prior experience, skill, needs, learning preferences and so on. If this spread is generally towards the better side of the scoring, it will usually reflect good training and a good trainer. If, however, the spread is mainly on the lower side of the scoring, then the implication is that the training, or the trainer, or both were not satisfactory. In this latter case there is the obvious need for further evidence.

Long-term validation and evaluation can also offer evidence which supports any other views of the effectiveness of the trainer. The emphasis of these approaches is on the training, so the comments made earlier will apply once more. Long-term training assessment has the objective of measuring the value of the training in terms of its direct application to work and the improvements in that work which should result. In many ways this type of evaluation is even more difficult than direct training validation and in most cases is highly subjective. The learners and their bosses may say that the changes over the period between the training and the evaluation contract are a result of the training, and they certainly may be, but the working environment has many other possible influences on learning and practice. At least at this stage, any end-of-course euphoria or otherwise will have faded and what the learner remembers about the training, say 6 months or a year after the training will be recall of a significant event or events.

Even this critical memory identification has its hazards. Even though the training may have been good and the trainer a satisfactory medium for this training, the 'significant' aspects remembered may not be the principal ones intended for retention. I recently met a manager who had attended one of my training courses, 16 years ago. His principle memory was of a particularly emotive activity I ran during the course – a memory of the emotive aspects of the activity and the functional nature of the activity rather than the lessons which had been drawn from it. This reaction is quite common and many trainers have been very disappointed that something they thought had been highly impactive did not seem to have registered, unfortunately, one of the frustrations of training. Simply because they do not say that they learned from an event, however, does not mean that there was no learning; often quite the contrary, and this becomes evident in many other ways than a spoken or written statement.

Long-term evaluation is usually undertaken as a follow-up some 6 or 12 months after the training, by means of either a written questionnaire or an interview.

Evaluation questionnaires

The questionnaire can often usefully be the same one used for the end-of-course validation, which enables a direct comparison to be made between the two – one completed immediately, the other with consideration and practice. The type of training may not, however, lend itself to this type of repetitive approach, but whether it does or not, there will be additional, essential questions. These will be about the application of the learning during the period reviewed – the implementation of the Action Plan completed at the end of the training.

In addition to the training evaluation questionnaire, this is an occasion when a special questionnaire can also be included relating directly to the learner's views about the trainer. A questionnaire could be offered at the end of the training, but we have already considered the potential dangers of one at that stage. Away from the training and in the 'safer' atmosphere of the learner's own workplace, he might be more likely to make an honest assessment of the trainer's capabilities. Of course, even this might be clouded because he is due to return to the training centre for another course with the same trainer the following week! At least, this is another piece of information to compare with and support other approaches.

Evaluation interviews

An alternative to the evaluation questionnaire is a visit of an assessor to interview the learner, and usually also his manager or supervisor, at their workplace. This can occur at the same time as a questionnaire would have been sent, or can follow the completion of questionnaires to clarify and confirm the responses. There are very strong arguments why the interviewer should be someone other than the trainer who conducted the training event. This ensures a degree of neutrality, although there is the danger that the interviewer does not have as complete an understanding of the training and its objectives as the trainer. On balance, the neutral interviewer would seem to be the most appropriate, especially in an attempt to assess the trainer's effectiveness. The learner, particularly at this later evaluation stage, is perhaps more likely to make comments about the trainer to someone other than the trainer, although there is no absolute guarantee that this will be so.

Discussion

The pre-assessment meeting
This meeting and its importance has already been mentioned: a meeting (or meetings) in which the assessor will be finding out as much as possible about the attitudes and knowledge of the trainer; his and the organization's objectives for the training; and an indication of the methods which the trainer will use during the event. The assessor may agree to be present throughout the event if this is necessary for the assessment – many courses cannot be viewed in segments. Or the assessor will agree, having learned about the course content and format in detail, to look at certain elements only of the event.

It is a foolish but common practice for assessors to believe that all they need do is, for example, to go into a course and observe without any prior discussion. This is a practice to be avoided if at all possible because it limits severely the basis against which the assessment will be made.

A pre-meeting has, of course, some dangers itself which the assessor should be aware of and avoid. By meeting beforehand with the trainer, the assessor gives the trainer the opportunity, by whatever means – personality, position, knowledge – to influence the assessor one way or another before the direct assessment.

The assessment meeting

Another useful discussion event which can provide supplementary evidence to be used in the assessment is the post-training meeting between the assessor, the trainer, the peer assessor, if used, and the learners' end-of-course assessment questionnaire on the trainer if one has been used. At this meeting all the information is pooled in the most open way possible and discussed. The discussion will centre principally around any differences in assessment between the contributing parties and will attempt to resolve these to improve the training and the trainer's contribution.

The discussion can also give the assessor further information about the trainer in terms of his acceptance of criticism, the ability to change and the motivation to make these changes, and perhaps an indication of his wider knowledge of 'new' techniques and methods suggested by the assessor.

There is a further side product in that, if a peer assessor is also involved, this might be a trainer whom the assessor is also about to assess. The contributions made by this individual during the discussion may give the assessor some advance information about him!

Observation

Both the supplementary evidence and the discussions are valuable as supportive approaches, but in the final analysis direct observation of the trainer in action is essential as the principal means of assessment of effectiveness. But simply sitting watching is not sufficient.

The value of the pre-training discussion in determining what the training and trainer's objectives, methods, attitudes and approaches are has been considered. Direct observation of events will test out the real meaning of these aims and objectives. A logical and structured

155

approach to the observations is needed, otherwise important factors may be omitted.

The main requirements in the observation of a training event are to know:

- What type of training you have to assess;
- Which aspect of that training you want/need to assess;
- What the objectives of that training might be;
- Which methods, techniques and approaches does the trainer intend to use;
- What levels or standards you will be using to compare;
- How many times and over which period you will observe;
- What type(s) of instrument, if any, you will use as an observational aid?

Comments have been made on all these factors in earlier sections of this book, but some additional comments are necessary on the questions of standards and also the instruments to be used.

Standards

Possible means of describing the standards required of a trainer in various circumstances were described in Chapter nine – identification of needs; identification of skill levels against job needs (the Trainer Task Inventory); and a comprehensive description of competence standards required. The latter description, when available in its completed form will be very useful indeed to assessors because it will not only identify the areas which should be assessed, but will also offer indicators with which to assess. The standards can be modified as necessary to suit the range of trainers involved and therefore it will be possible to determine the competence levels in the task which are being performed to the required levels. The one problem will be in fact identifying these 'required levels', although the standards will give a good indication of these. The levels will need to be identified for the specific situation being assessed, and although any measuring instrument appears to be objective, it must be remembered that much of the assessment will be subjective assessment against subjective items.

Sometimes the determination of levels will be relatively easy – the case of the trainee gas meter reader who during training was required to learn how to read 100 meters in one hour with 100 per cent accuracy. Assessment of this achievement is easy and the skill of the trainer in performing the necessary training will show readily in the results. This will be the case with many mechanical, systematic and procedural types of jobs and the training associated with them.

In other cases, the levels will be subjective and might be 'measurable' only against:

- Accepted models of behaviour;
- A standard set by an 'authority'; for example, the competence standards set by the Lead Body for Training and development;
- An organization or company defined standard.

The problems can be seen readily if attempts are made to define levels and standards for an interpersonal skills workshop and the trainer or facilitator involved in this. What is the measure of success? How is it measured? Can it be measured? and so on.

Whatever the problems may be, a level must be determined and agreed. In practice it must be possible to apply it consistently across the occupation, company or sector of training. The assessor must always be aware of these levels and what they mean, particularly the highly subjective ones, because his personal values may change with changing circumstances.

12

Trainer assessment inventories

Instruments for observation

If an event or a series of events, perhaps with a number of trainers, is to be observed, the assessor must have something on which to record his observations and resulting views. Typical instruments for the supplementary validation of training have already been considered. The instruments now in question relate directly to observation of the *trainer*. It is doubtful whether it is possible to construct a realistic instrument for use in the observation of all activities of a trainer, but, equally, these should be kept to a minimum otherwise their numbers would make their use confusing or undesirable.

The criteria for which instruments to use will depend on the type of training and what it involves. Trainers of all kinds will be involved in:

- Input sessions or presentations of material;
- Discussion sessions as separate events or as integral parts of another type of event;
- The control of activities, games, exercises and role plays and the control of the feedback and appraisal of these events;
- Demonstrations of actual tasks or operations.

Most of the activities of trainers will be confined to these four areas. Other activities can probably be measured using only variations of the instruments.

The assessor and producer of observational instruments must remember that the purpose of the observation is to consider the effectiveness of the processes, techniques and the methods employed by the trainer, not the content of the task, unless this is so inappropriate that it affects the training process. For example, if the information given in an input session is so out of date that the trainer loses credibility with the group and also loses control of them, the content is relevant in the assessment of the trainer as well as the training.

Presentation skills

A superficial look to the observation and assessment of a trainer giving a presentation, a lecture, or a talk to what I refer to as an input session, would seem to suggest that this is a simple task. However, it is in this area, in which every trainer works to a greater or lesser degree for some period of his job, where there are so many factors to assess.

The way in which the training is received by the assessor and the learners can only be a matter of personal judgement perhaps weighted by:

• Your learning preferences;
• Your interpersonal reaction to the behaviour of the trainer;
• The charisma or otherwise of the trainer;
• The level of your interest in the subject;
• The level of your needs to learn about the subject;
• The methods, novel or otherwise, of the presentation;

and so on.

Because all these variants exist, how will a consistent approach ever be possible? The answer is – with difficulty, but aided by a full realization of the difficulties and subjectivity associated with assessment.

Assessment of the trainer in the input session will be a personally accepted model of behaviour in the form of:

1. A universally accepted model of presentation skills;
2. A consistent personal model;
3. A model or approach decreed by the culture or the organization.

In most cases the approach will be a mixture of 1. and 2., although many organizations still impose specific requirements and constraints on their presenters – the trainer or other speaker will sit/stand/be still/move about, speak from a lectern/be formally dressed all the time/be casually dressed, etc.

The basic model of assessment will usually include consideration of whether the trainer has taken account of the many environmental requirements; uses effective verbal and non-verbal behaviours; includes the effective use of aids – visual, audio and video – and develops an interpersonal relationship with the learning group. As suggested above these may all vary considerably with the situation, but will all be included on any occasion in some form.

Environmental requirements

Many of these may be outside the control of the trainer, but the assessor must confirm this, rather than assume that nothing could have been done.

The following items could be included in assessment:

- Room comfort. Has the trainer taken the size of the room, the type of seating and the air conditioning into account in his planning of where the training should take place? Is the extraneous noise level sufficiently low to avoid distracting the learners? If the training is taking place in a hotel, has the piped 'musak' or announcements been silenced? Are the main training rooms and any supplementary rooms of a satisfactory size and nature?
- Personal comfort. Is the training accommodation of a sufficient size for the number of learners and the nature of the training? What arrangements for smoking/non-smoking have been made? Are the refreshment and meal breaks organized and known to the learners? Are the starting and finishing times of the training day (if possible) known to the learners? Are the starting and finishing times of the sessions (if possible) known to the learners? Have arrangements been made for the ending of the event to allow learners' travelling needs to be taken into account?
- Other factors. If there is a telephone in the training room, has this been disconnected? Have arrangements been made with the administration to avoid interruptions, except in emergency, during the training periods? Were all the administration arrangements carried out efficiently – correspondence, call-up papers, receipt of precourse material, training programme, provision of all equipment and stationery required for the event?
- General. Did the trainer have a checklist for these items or did he rely on memory? Which was desirable in this situation?

Presentational behaviours

These relate to the actual skills of presentation exhibited by the trainer and include both his verbal and non-verbal skills of presentation. Items which would be included in the assessment observation are:

161

General observable behaviour

Did the trainer exhibit nervousness at the start of and during the session? Was this nervousness excessive? Did the nervousness reduce as the session progressed? Was the session content relevant, up to date, accurate, of the level required and sufficiently comprehensive?

Verbal behaviour

Was the voice volume appropriate to the size of the room and the group? Was the vocabulary used appropriate to the learning group? Was jargon used which could not be understood? Did the trainer appear to try to impress the learners by using training jargon terms and references? Did the trainer have a local accent too strong to be understood by the range of learners present? Was the material presented in an acceptable or, for example, a patronizing way? Was the presentation free from too many verbal habits or idiosyncrasies? Was humour used effectively? Was the humour always inoffensive in such matters as language, race, sex, religion, disablement and other minority groups?

Non-verbal behaviour

Most language experts agree that:

1. People react more to what we do and how we say things than to what we actually say;
2. About 70% of effective communication is made via non-verbal communication rather than through verbal communication;
3. The verbal communication and the non-verbal communication must be congruent, that is to say in step with each other, otherwise the result is misunderstanding and/or suspicion.

The trainer is very sensitive to the effects of non-verbal communication because in his exposed position everybody can easily see all his body language. A learner or member of an audience who displays unacceptable behaviours may be unseen in a crowd, but the person addressing that crowd is on show to all. The trainer must not forget that he is exposed to view.

Are there any irritating habits – money jangling, key rattling, pencil playing, finger jabbing – which distract the learner from the training message? Does the trainer have good eye contact with the group? Is the eye contact shared with all the group rather than one or two members or one section of the group only? Does the trainer have visual habits which might be distracting – looking over the heads of the group at the clock at the back of the room, all the time, looking out of the window while he is talking? Are there any non-verbal sound habits which may tempt the learners to count them rather than listen to the training message – the grunts, 'yeahs', 'ems', 'mmms'? To what extent is any nervousness allowed to show in the trainer's behaviour – perspiration, voice loss, rapid breathing, forgetting words?

Visual, audio and video aids

The trainer who can succeed completely by talking alone is very rare indeed and requires a *very* strong charisma even to hope to succeed. Even charisma palls after a while. Apart from varying the presentation in order to encourage interest, the use of aids to speech encourages learning – if we are able to see something we more easily learn it than by hearing about it alone. Some verbal descriptions without a picture or the object itself are meaningless. The use of training aids can be used to support the verbal messages of the trainer.

When training aids are mentioned the usual reaction is to think of the ubiquitous overhead projector and its acetate slides, and the equally well-known flipchart – simple visual aids equipment and material. Simplicity should not be rejected however, because more trainers have succeeded in putting across their message using these two simple aids than those who have attempted to be very clever in their presentations and use a host of complicated equipment.

Overhead projector (OHP) slides can be used more adventurously than is usually the case. With a little extra preparation a simple OHP slide can have a great impact. All that is required is the imaginative use of colour, shapes and sizes in addition to the normal words. Does the trainer attempt to improve his slides in this way?

Slides are often more effective if parts of them are disclosed progressively rather than showing the complete slide on the screen all the time. This can be achieved simply by using a piece of paper and moving it down the slide (put it underneath the slide so that the images/words can be seen); or hinged, card flaps can be laid over sections which can then be disclosed or hidden; or a number of part slides can be used to build up to the complete slide by adding them on top of each other. Does the trainer stick to the traditional method of displaying information, or does he attempt to use novel methods?

Even the simple acetate roll often found fixed to OHPs can be used more adventurously than by writing on the exposed part then rolling it on to await the next entries. The roll can be prepared with a series of slides drawn sequentially on it. This is useful if the series is always used and in that order, although it does hinder flexibility. A roll can tell a story with almost cinematic images as the roll is turned, and perhaps accompanied by music or a recorded commentary. Gimmicky? Perhaps, but these and other 'different' approaches can support and increase the facility for learning. Does the trainer experiment or is he only willing to 'do what everybody has always done'.

163

The flipchart is generally regarded as the trainer's universal work-horse. It is easily mobile, can be set up and used under almost any conditions and is very flexible in use. Sheets can be prepared before the event for progressive disclosure in a sequence, or even an interrupted or modified sequence. Or they can be written on as the session progresses. Does the trainer use pre-prepared charts and posters, and if so are they well-prepared and readable? Can he find the pre-prepared sheets readily among the blank sheets? Are the sheets imaginatively completed, yet clear and understandable? Is the writing intelligible? Are colours, shapes and sizes used imaginatively? Are the flipchart sheets clean and attractive rather than dirty and dog-eared?

One of the more usual uses of the flipchart is to record during sessions the views of the learners, perhaps as a result of their individual or group considerations of a question posed by the trainer. When taking comments from the learners, does the trainer write clearly; put down what is said rather than what he thinks (or wants) has been said; is everything recorded without selectively ignoring certain comments? Is the recorded information treated with respect when it has been made, rather than being crumpled up and thrown away (in full sight of the group)?

Does the trainer appear to be aware of the necessary conditions for constructing flipchart sheets? Does he know which sizes of lettering will be visible in different rooms? Does he seem to be aware of the different visual values of different colours? Does he use symbols, diagrams, images in addition to words?

Audio aids

Before the advent of simple video recording, the audio cassette recorder was the only 'home recording' aid. It was used to record practice interviews, talks, etc, which are now recorded on closed-circuit television, if available. The audio cassette and recorder still has a place in training as it is cheap, although it is not as flexible and does not have the same impact as video. Presentations can be varied by playing short pieces of pre-recorded information, either by the trainer or some other known person. They can include either part or all of an audio-visual package to support or supplement the presentation. Does the trainer appear to be aware of the possible uses of audio? If he uses them, does he use them as imaginatively as he could? Does he know how to get the best out of the equipment? What happens if the equipment goes wrong? Is it apparent that he checked the equipment prior to the session? Did he ensure that everybody could hear the sound?

Video/film aids

Like much of the general population, many trainers, look on videos as simply an updated form of the 35mm films which were in common use in training 10 to 15 years ago. However, they differ in format, require a different equipment, and the methods and techniques for using them are quite different. Apart from anything else they are much more portable and easier to operate than film – even when the film projector has automatic loading.

As far as training and development is concerned, the major difference is in their use. Some trainers have not converted from films to videos and use the videos as though they were films. The traditional way of viewing a film – even in training – has been to watch it through completely, then hold a post-film discussion. This was encouraged by the potential problems of keeping on stopping and starting a 35mm sprocket-holed film, even on projectors with pause mechanisms. Too much interruption would be likely to result in problems with the projector and/or the film.

Video cassettes are constructed in a different way and with present day, state-of-the-art video players, they almost cry out for interruption. Instead of watching from beginning to end, interruptions can be made a number of times during a video, with mini-discussions at each natural stage. In fact a number of training video producers are now making videos with this intention and either introduce gaps at stopping points, or construct the scenario into natural break segments which give the trainer the options of stopping or carrying on.

There can be of course problems with interrupted viewing. If the interruptions are too numerous, and are not natural ones, the cry can be 'Oh no, not again', causing antagonism against the video and the potential learning.

Does the trainer introduce the video effectively and smoothly? If the video has to be started at a point other than the beginning, was this prepared in advance? Is the interruption technique used effectively, or are videos always played straight through? Is the video the most appropriate technique for the event? Does the video fit into the presentation, or does it interfere? Is the trainer at ease in operating the video equipment? Is it evident that the trainer is knowledgeable about the video content? Does he easily introduce discussion at the appropriate points?

General issues

Can the trainer control the beginnings and endings of the presentations? After all, a bad start can ruin what would have otherwise been an effective presentation. Similarly, a bad ending can undo or detract from all the good work previously achieved. Has the trainer pitched the material at the right level for the learner group? How well does he stick to his allotted time? Is all the intended material included, or did any important issues have to be omitted because of an overestimation of the amount of material, or an underestimation of time? To what extent did the 'Must,' 'Should' and 'Could know' control the pattern of the presentation?

Assessment inventories

A suggested inventory for use when assessing a presentation is given in Appendix One. This is the first in a small series presented here which can be produced for use within any organization by modifying the entries according to the situation and the assessment needs. A set of guidelines is also included at the start of this assessment guide, but not repeated for each guide for reasons of space.

This type of inventory can be used in a variety of ways and assessors will, through experiment, find the way which suits them most. Whichever approach is used, assessors will find it useful to:

1. Familiarize themselves fully before the event with all the assessment aspects included (a checklist is included with the inventory);
2. Use the inventory during the event rather than rely completely on memory. To what extent the inventory is completed during the event will depend on the assessor's approach. Some will find it convenient to make entries in the comments spaces only, leaving the ratings to be completed afterwards; others may wish to rate the items during the event and add comments at their leisure later; others will wish to complete the full inventory during the event; and yet others will wish to use only the checklist with free notes, and complete the full inventory after the event.

The types of variation possible within the instruments shown in the appendices include principally content and rating scales. The content will vary according to the particular type of event and also the specific needs of the assessor. Assessment can be approached from a positive or a negative viewpoint, and although positive approaches are more satisfactory psychologically, they are often more difficult to assess. For example, in Appendix 1, the first question relates to the nervousness of the presenter at the start of the presentation. The positive viewpoint would suggest looking at his confidence shown at the start of the presentation, rather than his nervousness. The decision as to which approach should be used must of course rest with the assessor who has to be comfortable with the assessments used. I find it easier when assessing to look for the failings initially – these are usually much more evident than the successes. If failings are being looked for, but they are not evident, then the other end of the scale reflects the positive viewpoint that success is there rather than failure.

However, how would I recognize confidence? When we say we are looking for signs of confidence, most observers will rate a presenter as confident usually 'because they do not exhibit signs of nervousness', but this will depend on whether the assessor is perfectly clear what he is looking for.

The rating scales in the appendices have five scoring divisions. I find that I am usually best able to work with seven. Many assessors, however, find that a division into seven levels of skill is too many to cope with, but they find five levels acceptable. Others find that even five levels are either too difficult or not realistic. Consequently they prefer a three scale rating approach.

Similarly many people find it difficult to accept an odd number of rating scales – 5 or 7 – because they feel that others treat the 3 or 4 score as 'average'. Consequently they prefer a 4 or 6 scale for rating. If this suits you better than a 5 or 7 scale, by all means use the one with which you feel most comfortable. The principal criterion must be that scoring on whatever scale must be as meaningful as possible.

Another area which has links with the first variation discussed above relates to the apparent or real subjectivity of the 'measure'. An example of this is 'sincerity'. Some people argue that because sincerity is an emotion or feeling, it cannot really be observed and assessed, and therefore should not appear in an assessment instrument. If the assessor feels that he cannot recognize apparent sincerity, then it should be excluded. Many aspects of assessment of people performing fall into the subjective category. What we must beware of is *interpreting* the behaviour of the trainer being assessed. All we can go on is the observable behaviour; anything else is dangerous. I accept that it is highly subjective, but if I am listening to and watching a trainer presenting a session, I may have a feeling whether or not that trainer is being sincere. This is based on whether his behaviour comes over to me that he is being sincere in the things he is saying or doing. It doesn't matter whether he is sincere or not – as long as his overt behaviour appears consistently sincere to me. Some observers may not be able to recognize overt sincere or insincere behaviour. If this is so and they recognize this inability (and they may be being more honest about their abilities than those of us who claim to be able to recognize sincere behaviour), then this category of assessment must be excluded.

Whichever method is used, the assessor will usually be making some notes during the event. Although this must be performed openly, it must not be *too* apparent, otherwise the trainer's performance might be affected. The main problem encountered by assessors in using these inventories is in determining the standards for the ratings. This can only be achieved using one of the universally accepted 'models', which were described earlier.

Discussion leading skills assessment

Assessment of the trainer's discussion leading skills will be necessary when he leads discussions, either as separate events in a training programme, or as integral parts of an input session. Whichever discussion activity is being considered, the techniques are the same and show standard type of leader behaviour for this activity.

The main role for the trainer in discussions with the learners will be one of initiator and then controller of the discussion, rarely the principal contributor to the event. Did the trainer lead the discussion or did he take it over? How was the discussion introduced? How was the event handled if the discussion emerged naturally? Were the learners clear about what they were to discuss? Were the objectives of the discussion made clear to the learners?

If the discussion is to be a significant event in its own right, rather than part of another event, the initiating trainer will have to prepare for the discussion in the same way that he prepared for an input session. Was the trainer's approach clear and determined? Had the trainer a shopping list or agenda for the discussion? How obvious was the use of aids? Did the trainer start the discussion with a visual/audio aid of some nature? Had the trainer prepared questions to inject if the discussion ran out of steam?

During the discussion the trainer will put questions and listen carefully to the discussion. What kind of questions did the trainer pose? How appropriate were they? Did they help or hinder the discussion? Did the trainer give time for the learners to consider the question before replying? Did the trainer show he was listening to the learners' contributions? How did he demonstrate this?

The third role of the trainer is to end the discussion or see that it is ended in a clear and positive manner, and that the objective has been achieved and necessary action agreed. To what extent were summaries used during the discussion? Was there a comprehensive summary at the end of the discussion? Who was responsible for making the summaries? Were the summaries always clear and comprehensive, and to what extent did the trainer ensure that this was so? To what extent were the learners allowed/encouraged to express their satisfaction or otherwise with the discussion? Was the discussion controlled so that it was contained within the time allocated?

The assessor will be aware that a discrete discussion session is to take place and be observed, that there is the intention to include a discussion within a specific input session, or that during an input session a discussion is likely to start up. He will therefore ensure that there is an appropriate observation instrument to hand, particularly in the last-mentioned case. A suggested discussion leading observation inventory is shown at Appendix Two.

Activities, games, exercises, role plays

Many training events include a number of practical activities, which may be games designed for specific skill purposes – decision making, problem saving, negotiation and so on – and people care games such as action mazes. Activities may take the form of syndicate or group exercises, in which learners in the groups take on roles, solve problems as a group, exhibit effective group behaviour, and so on. Role plays are either of imaginary or real-life situations, and these may be observed by the trainer and their colleagues, either directly or via CCTV. The role events may also take place, not as pre-determined activity in the training event, but as a 'hot' role play which arises naturally during discussion/activity of a real-life problem. This can be developed into an immediate role play with the initiators of the situation 'living' the situation. If the problem is one which has been brought to the training by one of the learners, the originator of the problem may play themselves or the person with whom they were in conflict, or even, on some occasions, both parties, as in the 'empty chair' approach.

Whatever the practical event might be, there are likely to be common factors, for the activity must be introduced, briefings must be given either orally or from written instructions, and all the arrangements made for the activity to proceed. During the activity the trainer, in addition to arranged observers, will observe the process, usually with little or no intervention. After the event the participants, the observers and the trainer will discuss what has happened, the process, the behaviours, the results and give feedback from their different viewpoints.

In activities of this nature, the trainer might play one or more of a number of roles. But the event has to be initiated. Did the trainer present the activity clearly? Did the trainer ensure that the participants were clear about what was expected of them? Were written/oral briefs clear and comprehensive, but constrained in extent and complexity?

169

Was it made clear how much time was allocated to the event? If leaders were appointed, did they know who their group members were, and did the group members know who their leader was? Were clear location instructions given? Were syndicate, sub-group activity rooms prepared?

During the activity the trainer's role can be that of interventionist or the deliberate non-interventionist. The former can interrupt the group while it is performing an activity when he sees them either going along a path which will lead to failure, or they are not bringing out the lessons he wanted to emerge, or they are taking up too much time on a non-essential part, and so on. There is always the likelihood that the group will:

- Accept the lead and do only what is obviously expected of them;
- Reject the lead and go ahead as they want to do;
- Reject the lead and come into conflict with the trainer;
- Accept the help gratefully.

The problem in all of these reactions, even the last mentioned, is that much of the resulting activity is dictated by the trainer and consequently the learning by the group may be minimal or non-existent.

The alternative approach is when the trainer withdraws from active participation, having started the activity, and deliberately does not intervene whatever the provocation. There must then be total non-intervention. However much the group might appeal to the trainer to help them, or he sees problems arising for the group; he must resist the temptation. Of course, if the safety of the group is involved then he must intervene, but the intervention must be the last resort. Part of a group's real learning occurs when they find, because of a decision they have made, they have gone wrong and have to make further decisions to solve the problem. What kind of strategy does the trainer adopt? How well does he stick to it? How appropriate is the strategy for the situation? Does he intervene at appropriate times? Even though he has a non-intervention strategy, does he intervene when it is essential for him to do so?

As important as the activity itself is the post-activity discussion, intended to extract all the learning points which emerged during the activity. The format of this discussion will depend on the type of activity. Following an exercise or game, the feedback is often given mainly by the observers who have been briefed to look at certain parts of the activity process and structure, and the behaviour of the participants, particularly the appointed leader. In addition, the feelings and reactions of the participants themselves can be sought. Finally, the trainer can make a contribution if there is anything left to say, certainly in picking up the pieces and preparing the participants for the next activity.

In role plays the trainer will also be responsible for controlling the feedback and appraisal, taking an active part only if significant aspects or learning points have been missed, or to present an alternative viewpoint. Otherwise the trainer will probably be leaving the main appraisal in, say, a face-to-face interview role play, to the interviewer and the interviewee with supporting comments by the observers.

Did the trainer explain the appraisal/feedback system clearly? Did the trainer encourage the participants and the observers to take the feedback roles? To what extent did the trainer contribute to the appraisal? Was this contribution relevant and appropriate? To what extent did the trainer 'take over' the appraisal? How necessary was this? Did the trainer allow an ineffective or inaccurate feedback to go unchallenged? How was the challenge raised? Was CCTV used in the feedback? Was this used effectively? Was creative use made of any CCTV facility?

An example of an observational inventory for this type of trainer and training event is shown in Appendix Three.

Demonstrations

A common procedure, particularly in mechanical, technical and procedural training, is for the real object, device or system to be used during the training as the most effective means of making the training realistic. In such cases the object will need to be described and demonstrated, and opportunities given for the learners to have 'hands-on' practice and experience of the object. Such a 'demonstration' must be performed in an interesting and effective way, or else an important opportunity for a live training experience will be lost. The description 'demonstration' includes not only the description, display and demonstration of the object by the trainer, but also the opportunity for the learners to demonstrate their learned ability.

Has the trainer made example(s) of the subject available? Is there opportunity for hands-on practice by the learner? Does the trainer ensure that everybody has an opportunity to practice? Does the trainer ensure that the learners really understand what they are doing and why?

An observation inventory suitable for this kind of event is given at Appendix Four.

Other observations

The four inventories described above do not exhaust the types of observational instruments available for use. Earlier, Behaviour Analysis was described as a very suitable instrument for observing, recording and analysing behaviour. This is used mainly with training groups themselves, but a Behaviour Analysis form can easily be constructed to be used in the observation of specific behaviours by the trainer in a number of situations. Other activity analysis forms, similar to Behaviour Analysis but concentrating on the use of structure, can be developed for special occasions. Most observation assessment purposes will normally be covered by one or more of the four inventories described, either in the form shown in the Appendices or modified to suit the particular types of occasion.

Some assessors prefer a combined inventory when a training session being observed includes, for example, a lecture with a discussion and also an activity. The three inventories can, of course, be used, but Appendix Five shows how the assessment items can be combined into one document. Activities common to the three parts of the session have been identified, followed by questions specific to the parts of the session. The guides can be combined in other ways depending on the type of inventory required.

Trainee assessment

The approach with the highest risk factor and the potentially lowest realistic result is to ask the learners to complete an end-of-course assessment on the trainer, in addition to the usual one on the training. The euphoric factor has already been mentioned, as well as the opposite effect when the learners have not gelled with the trainer. At the end of an event, common sense is not likely to prevail over natural, perhaps strong emotions. However, the learners have been directly on the receiving end of the trainer's actions and relationship with them, and although they may not be in the best position to comment, it is possible that even out of emotive statements some realism might emerge. So asking them to complete an assessment is not a complete waste of time and may in fact produce some useful results. If it is obvious that there has been a high degree of euphoria, the assessor must look carefully to see whether they are reacting only to a charismatic trainer. On the other hand, if the mood is depressive, what has gone wrong? To what extent has the trainer's lack of skills contributed or even caused this?

The answer must lie of course in using the learners' comments in parallel with the observations of the assessor and others. This suggests that the most appropriate occasion on which to seek learner assessments is when other observations are being made – it is dangerous to use the trainee assessments alone. The comments of the learners will be principally at the reactive, rather than the considered level. The learners will be applying immediate reaction rather than a delayed consideration based on learning needs, methods, techniques and styles. Many trainers have had the experience of their learners leaving the course dissatisfied with them, yet on meeting them some time later they have admitted they learned a great deal, and time and consideration has shown them that what happened was essential to the learning process. They should have been disgusted with themselves rather than the trainer for their reactions – this of course was all part of the learning.

If the learners are to be asked to make a trainer assessment, any request must be kept short and simple, particularly if they are also being asked to complete a training validation questionnaire. The trainer assessment questionnaire must be introduced carefully and openly, giving the learners every opportunity for anonymity.

The format in Appendix Six is a suggested one which can be modified easily depending on the circumstances and in correspondence with the assessor's approach.

The observation and assessment guides reproduced in the Appendices will not guarantee that assessment is made easy, nor that common standards will result, but they will go a long way towards achieving these aims by providing consistent means of observing and recording. The differences between the people who might assess – their personal values and skills in judgement – will always mean that 100 per cent consistency will never be possible. If the formats suggested are used, the differences can be demonstrated and discussed.

13

Costs and plans

If observation inventories of the types described in the previous chapter are used to assess a trainer in action, and this assessment shows that the trainer is effective and the training is valid, the employing organization can be reasonably sure that it is receiving value for most of its money. The assessment of the monetary value of training and trainers can be as subjective and as difficult as the validation of some of the forms of training previously mentioned. If attempts are made to extend this cost or value analysis to include monetary levels in the overall evaluation, the difficulties become even more evident.

Cost-value analysis must be part of the assessment of a trainer once his actual training abilities have been confirmed, otherwise the organization will have no idea, for example, how many trainers it must employ to perform the training desired. How much is a trainer worth? What is the total, net cost of the training to the organization? What is the cost of a training day? How many trainers/training days can the organization afford?

In order to assess these values, the assessor must be able to attribute a cost to everything connected with the training – this is easier said than done!

The costs of training

The costs attributable to the training function can be divided into three main sections:

1. Fixed costs relating to the training establishment;
2. Supportive costs in respect of (a) trainers, (b) learners;
3. Opportunity costs.

Fixed costs

Fixed costs include those which are reasonably regular and fixed over a period of time, say a year. They can comprise:

1. Salaries, insurance and pensions contributions for the training manager and the training officers; administrative staff; guest speakers (in this latter case only a proportion of their costs could be attributed to the training, the proportion related to their input to the training).
2. Cost of the training accommodation in terms of yearly rates, water rates, capital equipment (e.g. furniture, cabinets, etc.) and cleaning and regular maintenance costs. This accommodation would include the training manager's office, any office accommodation allocated to the trainers, administration staff space and of course accommodation used for training;
3. Electricity, gas, oil, telephone costs attributable to the training function.

Supportive costs

Costs incurred for (a) the trainers and (b) the learners are called support costs. They occur less frequently than fixed costs and can include:

1. a. External accommodation costs for the training and the trainers – training room hire, equipment hire, bedroom and meals costs for the trainers in hotels and conference centres;
    b. Travelling and out-of-pocket subsistence costs for the trainers;
    c. Equipment, books and aids purchase and other provision and maintenance.

2. a. Accommodation costs for the learners;
    b. Travelling and other subsistence costs for the learners;
    c. The learners' salaries.

Opportunity costs

Although learners' salaries which have been included in the above costing summary, are paid while the learner is away on the training course, the learners are not directly contributing to the company output. The value of this non-contribution is often described as the

176

'opportunity' cost – the value of that individual's services if he had been contributing directly in his job to the company output. In many ways this will have to be a subjective amount, although some companies claim that they are able to calculate this lost opportunity value accurately.

Evaluation

Even more subjective will be any attempts to link the overall value of an individual's training and development to an increase in work output, efficiency, higher earning value, etc. We have seen earlier that it is very difficult, if not impossible, to attribute a value to the total learning process. Few attempts have been made, and these are little more than intelligent guesses. Trained people who are involved in direct operation tasks can have their efficiency assessed and, if they were unskilled before the training, then any increase in skill and the output value resulting can be attributed to the training. In most training cases, this is not possible. The problem is so great that organizations attempting to assess the cost of training simply ignore this factor. If it is consistently ignored comparisons can be made between one period and another, but it has to be accepted that a valuable part of the training function is being ignored.

Cost analysis

It is possible using the figures related to the costs summarized above to produce a monetary statement from which a number of conclusions can be drawn – cost of the training function; cost of the training function per individual; cost of the training per learner, and so on. These are useful within the constraints mentioned above. The main advantage I have found in using them has been in comparing them from one period to another. It does not matter too much if the figures are not completely accurate representations, provided the same calculations and methods of calculations are used on each occasion.

In the simplest analysis, a unit cost of training per trainer can be obtained by adding together all the known costs – fixed, support and opportunity. If this figure is divided by the number of people who contribute towards this training – the training manager, the training officers, the administration staff and the attributed external speakers – the resulting figure is one form of cost. For example, if the sum of all the costs is £250 000 per annum with a training function staff of eight, the unit cost per trainer is about £31 000. Of course, this calculation masks a number of factors – cost of external training and open learning (which would increase the cost per trainer), high course numbers (which should decrease the cost per trainer) and a value based on the evaluation of the training and transfer to work (which would further reduce the unit cost). Even without these other factors it at least gives a baseline measure which can be used as a comparative costing from one year to another, using the same sets of factors. If in the following year the total cost of the same factors has risen to £320 000, the cost per trainer will have increased to £40 000. If the general cost of living index had risen by 8 per cent, a simple increase to £270 000 would have occurred, however, the actual rise represents an increase of 28 per cent. There may be a good explanation for this rise on this occasion, but the additional 20 per cent increase requires some form of enquiry to be made.

Costing can be approached from another angle. If the total training cost is £250 000 in the one year and 3000 learners pass through 200 courses in that time, the cost per learner (in which of course the trainers have been involved) is £83 and the cost per course is £1250. If, using the increase in the example above, in the following year when the cost was £320 000, the number of learners was increased to 4200 and the courses to 300, but with the same training input, the relevant costing would decrease to £76 per learner and £1067 per course in spite of the previously demonstrated increase of 28 per cent!

It is also possible to cost the training in terms of the number of learners who have attended the events. One method by which course 'costs' can be reduced is to increase the number of participants on each course – costs of the trainer salaries and training accommodation, etc. remain the same, there is a small increase in the learner salary attribution, but the net result is a lower cost per learner. This effect is particularly noticeable when external providers are brought in to tutor courses. If for a five-day course the consultant's fee is £2500, all other factors remain more or less the same, but the learner unit cost reduces considerably with the increase in course participants. If the course population is normally eight, the unit learner cost is £312 related to the consultant fee. If the number is increased to 15, with only a relatively small increase in learner salary costs, the unit learner cost reduces to only £167.

When cost reductions are being considered for internally resourced or externally provided training by means of increased course participant numbers, care must be taken that in increasing these numbers the quality of the learning does not suffer.

The examples quoted above are all basic approaches to costing without taking into account the many plus and minus factors, especially if an attempt is made to use as a balancing figure the *value* of the training to the organization in terms of increased business and hence profits. Apart from the difficulty of using evaluation to try to produce a figure of this nature, it is almost impossible, except in the simplest of cases, to be absolutely sure that any improvement in performance has been in fact due to the training.

These problems do not suggest that there should be no attempts at costing, rather the reverse, but the problems must be recognized and care taken not to base too many decisions on costs alone.

Planning for assessment

By this stage in my description of how to approach the assessment of the effectiveness of trainers, the potential assessor will be starting to consider the trainer(s) he has to assess. The factors to be taken into account will include

- Where do the trainer's preferences lie?
- Do they show?
- How flexible is the trainer between the types?
- What type of training approach and attitude does the organization require?
- How flexible or capable of being influenced is the organization?
- What type of training has to be performed?
- Can the training format be modified?
- What needs to be assessed?
- Which is the most effective means of assessment in this case?
- What other approaches can be used in support?
- To what extent should other supportive approaches be used?
- How much assessment has to be done?
- Which inventories are available?
- Which inventories are the most suitable?

and so on.

This can be a bewildering set of choices, but decisions must be made and these will certainly be eased if there is a plan to follow. The plan proposed here has been followed in recent years by a number of organizations who:

1. Saw the need to have an assessment system for their trainers, and
2. Saw the need to plan the process to maximize assessor resources, minimize resource time and maximise effectiveness.

179

Planning flow chart

Some of the organizations have modified the plans to suit their particular requirements, others have followed the full plan, summarized in the flow chart in Figure 13.1.

One or two of the stages on the flow chart require comments. The remainder have all been adequately covered in the preceding text.

Stage 1

It will be seen from Figure 13.1 that one of the very early decisions to be made concerns who is to be responsible for making the assessments. The options available are:

1. *An external examining body* such as the voluntary training body (the successor to an Industrial Training Board – ITB) associated with the industry.
2. *An experienced and qualified external assessor*. This assessor need not have knowledge and experience in the specific industry, but must be skilled and knowledgeable in all matters of training and the assessment of trainers.
3. *The immediate line managers* of the trainers. These individuals may or may not have sufficient knowledge of training and assessment. If the line manager is a training manager he will probably, but not necessarily, have a wide training knowledge and skill in assessment. If so, no further particular action will be necessary. If, however, he has been training manager by title only, or is an operational line manager with a responsibility for training in his area, substantial training will be necessary. This will include training in:
- A wide knowledge build-up of training techniques, methods and approaches;
- The ability to identify good and bad training practices;
- Specific observation, assessment and feedback techniques;
- Counselling skills.

The method of providing the training for these line manager assessors will depend on the number to be trained. If only one or two are concerned it will be more economically viable for them to attend externally provided training events. If, however, a viable group can be formed with a minimum of, say, four assessors, a customized internal training event can be provided. This will be provided either by managers who are already skilled trainers and assessors (but not the trainers who are to be assessed themselves) or by an external training provider. This will be expensive, but the expense will be a once only investment in a group who will, hopefully, be able to carry out assessments over a number of years.

TRAINING SKILLS ASSESSMENT PLAN
FOR TRAINERS

1. *WHO IS TO ASSESS?*   Training manager and/or deputy and mentor trainer/senior trainer.

2. *WHO IS TO BE ASSESSED?*   Every trainer.
3. *WHAT TIME IS REQUIRED AND AVAILABLE?*   Number of trainers and level of skill = number of assessments/days/hours.

4. *WHEN (OVER WHAT PERIOD) IS THE ASSESSMENT TO*   Normally the appraisal year.
   TAKE PLACE
5. *WHERE IS THE ASSESSMENT TO BE UNDERTAKEN*   Wherever necessary
6. *PRODUCE A STATEMENT OF INTENT*
   6a. Obtain/provide comprehensive job description (Forward Plan)
   6b. Correlate job description with competences standards (or standards expected)
   6c. Obtain from organization any specific corporate demand
7. *MEET TRAINERS FOR INITIAL DISCUSSION*
   7a. Discussion of assessment plan
   7b. Confirmation by training manager and trainer of use of appropriate training modes
8. *DISCUSS AND AGREE MUTUAL EXPECTATIONS AND ARRANGEMENTS*
   With individual trainers agree assessment events with forward dates as far ahead as possible. Make these definite appointments.
   8a. Pre-training discussion
   8b. Observation of training events
   8c. Post-training discussion
9. *DISCUSS AND AGREE OPTIONAL ADDITIONAL ASSESSMENTS*
   9a. Parallel self-assessment
   9b. Parallel peer assessment
   9c. Parallel trainee assessment
10. *TAKE AGREED ASSESSMENT ACTION AS IN 8 & 9 ABOVE*
11. *ADDITIONAL SUPPORTIVE ANALYSES*
    11a. Analyse training validations
    11b. Make evaluation approaches or ensure availability of any evaluation results
    11c. Make evaluation visits or ensure availability of any visit results
12. *COMPLETE ASSESSMENT REPORTS AND OVERALL ASSESSMENT REPORT IN FORMAT DECIDED*
    12a. Interim reports on individual assessments
    12b. Overall report at end of assessment.

Figure 13.1 Planning flow chart

181

4. *A specially selected assessment group* drawn from within the company from individuals who have the necessary skills; who have some of the necessary skills and who can, with training, supplement these skills; who might benefit from taking on this part-time work as part of their career development; or simply those who have been identified as having, following training, the potential as assessors. The action necessary to bring them up to an effective level in assessment will depend on which category the individuals come from, and the needs will follow those described in 3. Similarly a training expense is almost certain to be incurred, but again this will be an initial expense only with the provision of a trained group of assessors.

Stage 6

At stage 6 in the planning process, the statements to be produced are concerned with a description of what the trainer should be doing, how he should be doing it, and so on, from both the viewpoints of effective training and any additional demands imposed by the organization – for example, trainer attitudes. As in any form of appraisal or assessment, the necessary starting point is the identification of what is required – it is obviously this against which the assessment of effectiveness is made. Otherwise the question is raised 'Effectiveness according to which standards?'. It is here that the existence of a comprehensive job description is essential. This must be more than cosmetic and must be amended to include as much fine detail as possible for use in the assessment. This will be the basis against which the assessment is made. If the description is incomplete, the assessment will be incomplete.

It is in this area of the assessment that the development competence standards described earlier will prove to be invaluable because of their attention to the detail of the important aspects of the trainer's job. The standards can be added to if necessary from the variations from the norm of the trainer's job or from the corporate requirements. It will also be seen that the standards statements also provide a considerable degree of help in providing assessment criteria by identifying performance criteria and performance indicators. If the Units and Elements of the standards statements are followed, there is an additional value to the trainer who will then be able to use the assessment of performance in accreditation for a National Vocational Qualification.

Stage 10

It is difficult to lay down hard and fast rules for how much assessment of an individual should be made. Much will depend on the individual and the assessments made after the start of the process. If the first assessment observation of a trainer in a lecture session suggests that he is an excellent presenter, the temptation is to accept that and require no further observation. It may be that time is short, but restricting observation is risky for a number of reasons. One of these is that the session observed may have been, unknown to the assessor, a speciality subject of that trainer. If he were to be observed presenting a completely different type of session, the assessment might not be as good. Even with the 'good' trainers, a minimum of three observations is therefore essential.

If the first observation suggests that there are a number of areas for improvement, these will naturally be discussed in the post-observation discussion with the trainer, and arrangements made for improvement. The trainer will then need to be observed again, following the action taken to make the improvements, and there will certainly need to be a third observation to confirm that all the changes have been consolidated.

If a trainer includes input sessions, discussion sessions, activity sessions and demonstrations in the course of a training event, it will be necessary for all these to be assessed to produce a final, complete assessment. This, of course, is the ideal, because it can represent a considerable investment of time in the observations alone, without any allied meetings and discussions. In practice therefore, the ideal may not be met, but as in everything it is something to be aimed for.

Stages 11a, 11b and 11c

Stage 11a is usually the examination by the assessor of the end-of-course validation inventories completed by the trainees which concentrate principally on the *training*, although as we have seen this can be an excellent indicator of the skill of the *trainer*. There is usually no need to examine and analyse every inventory for every course. A 20 per cent selection should give sufficient indication that all seems to be well, or that there may be problems due either to the training or the trainer. Again, analysis can be extended if the sample, at a suggested 20 per cent initial level, does not give all the information necessary.

Stage 11b must, because of timing, take place after the direct observation period and is linked with the 3, 6 or 12 months evaluation action taken by the trainer with the learners and their line managers. If this evaluation is performed by follow-up inventories, the assessor will need to analyse a percentage of the responses in the same way as the end-of-course inventories.

Stage 11c will ordinarily be a luxury, but might become important in the assessment if the inventories in stage 11b suggest that all is not well. It may then be necessary for the assessor to interview on their home ground the learners and their line managers to determine the full extent of the problem.

Stage 12

It will be a very useful part of the assessment exercise for the action taken and the results to be recorded; this of course will be essential in organizations which require a full written report from the assessor. A ring binder may be useful as a log book. In this the documents used in the assessment can be filed for reference – the updated, working document, job description and the competence standards statement (if any); any descriptive material produced by the assessor about the trainer resulting from his discussions with the trainer (and others) before the assessment proper; documents relating to the training to be assessed, and in particular statements of objectives and methods; completed inventories relating to the observations made by the assessor, trainer's peer and trainees; records of the post-observation discussions with agreements for action (the latter will be updated at the relevant times); analyses of end-of-course validations and any evaluation measures attempted.

This log book will then become a permanent record of that trainer for personnel use and as supportive material in the organization's appraisal system. It would be easy to say that this document should be open and available, not only to the assessor and the retainer of the log book – personnel and/or line manager – but also to the trainer. This may present some difficulties, although it should again be an ideal to be aimed at as long as its accessibility does not inhibit the assessor in reaching conclusions.

Conclusions

The warning comments at the end of Chapter 12 relating to the use of observational instruments, can also be applied to the use of plans for assessment. Complete success cannot be assured by the availability of a plan, however well conceived and executed, but it should enhance the likelihood of success as opposed to an indiscriminate attempt at assessment. Even if things go wrong during the action of the plan, it is usually easier to modify a plan to fit the changed circumstances than immediately to decide an action under duress. The plan may not fully succeed, but at least it will be possible to identify the failure and establish its cause.

Appendices

Trainer assessment guide

The purpose of the individual sections in each Trainer Assessment Guide, Appendices I to V, is to offer a rating scale, and, perhaps more importantly, space to make comments about why that rating was given. The rating scale used is a scale of 1 to 5, but this can be varied according to personal preferences – an even-number scale 1 to 4 or 6, or an odd-number scale 1 to 5 or 7.

Appendix V is a combined guide for a session which includes a lecture, a discussion and an activity. The most common observations have been combined and separate sections provided for each part of the session. Any of the sessions can be combined in this way as required.

Appendix VI is for use by learners to give information about their views of the skills of the trainer.

The 'Guidance for Use' notes are included here once only. However, they should precede each individual observational assessment guide.

Guidance for use

1. Familiarize yourself with the objectives of the session and discuss these with the trainer involved. Not every item in the notes will be used by every trainer on every occasion. You should concentrate on the appropriate ones.
2. Familiarize yourself with the subject headings in this assessment and be prepared to observe and note all those relevant.
3. Enter the rating numbers wherever you can, but remember that many of the behaviours will change during the session and you will need to make an overall assessment. For example, you can

rate immediately the section on 'Opening', but you will have to wait until later to rate the 'Continuation' section.

4. Circle the rating which you feel reflects most closely the trainer's behaviour and performance. Take account only of what you observe. A rating of '4' does not equate to any hypothetical 'average'; it represents a scoring level between '3' and '5'. If a word has to be associated with '4', this could be 'satisfactory'.

5. During the session maintain rough notes in order to enter final comments in the relevant spaces of the assessment guide. Again take account only of what you actually observe.

6. At all times try to be as objective as possible in your assessments, even though some of the assessments are subjective. Only assess what you observe, that is the overt behaviour of the person being assessed.

7. Use the spaces after each scoring scale as fully as possible to record your comments. Usually comments will be necessary only when the rating is less than good, but the spaces should also be used to mention particularly useful or effective techniques.

Appendix I

Lecture sessions

Checklist

1. Opening platform presence
2. Opening of session
3. Continuation of session
4. Eye contact (showing interest)
5. Sincerity
6. Enthusiasm
7. General manner
8. Voice
9. Visual aids
10. Visual aids relevance
11. Visual aids quality
12. Visual aids use
13. Subject coverage
14. Use of session notes
15. Use of questions
16. Response to questions
17. Learner involvement
18. Classroom control
19. Handouts – adequacy
20. Handouts 2 – relevance
21. Closing the session
22. Timing
23. Pace
24. Appropriate approach
25. Creativity
26. Overall rating
27. Any other comments

TRAINER ASSESSMENT GUIDE

Lecture Sessions

1. Opening platform presence
   To what extent did the trainer exhibit nervousness during the opening stages?
   None 1 2 3 4 5 A great deal
   How?

   How did they disappear as the session continued?
   Quickly 1 2 3 4 5 Not at all

2. Opening of session
   To what extent did the speaker obtain attention from the start?
   A great deal 1 2 3 4 5 Little
   How?

3. Continuation of the sessions
   To what extent did the speaker maintain attention as the session progressed?
   All the time 1 2 3 4 5 Lost it
   How?

4. Eye contact (showing interest)
   To what extent did the speaker maintain eye contact with the group?
   When Speaking
   Most of the time 1 2 3 4 5 Rarely
   In what way?

   When Listening
   Most of time 1 2 3 4 5 Rarely
   In what way?

5. Sincerity
   How sincere and committed to the subject did the speaker appear to be?
   Very 1 2 3 4 5 Not at all
   How did this show?

6. Enthusiasm
   How enthusiastic was the speaker's manner?
   Very 1 2 3 4 5 Not at all
   How was this evidenced?

7. General manner
   To what extent did the speaker's manner relax you and encourage you to listen?
   A great deal 1 2 3 4 5 Little
   What distracting mannerisms were present?

8. Voice
   How clear to the whole group was the speaker?
   Very clear 1 2 3 4 5 Unclear
   In unclear or tending towards unclear, in what way?

   How appropriate was the language used?
   Appropriate 1 2 3 4 5 Inappropriate
   If inappropriate or tending towards inappropriate, in what way?

9. Visual aids
   To what extent did the speaker use visual aids to vary the presentation?
   A great deal 1 2 3 4 5 None

10. Visual aids relevance
    How relevant to the training were the visual aids?
    Relevant 1 2 3 4 5 Not relevant
    In what way?

11. Visual aids quality
    What was the quality of the visual aids used?
    Excellent 1 2 3 4 5 Poor
    Why?

12. Visual aids use
    How effectively were the visual aids used?
    Very well 1 2 3 4 5 Badly
    How?

13. Subject coverage
    How well within the objectives was the subject covered?
    Completely 1 2 3 4 5 Poorly
    What was omitted or unclear?

14. Use of session notes
    Was the use of session notes distracting?
    Not at all 1 2 3 4 5 Very much
    In what way?

15. Use of questions
    How well did the speaker use questions to the group?
    Very well 1 2 3 4 5 Badly
    How?

16. Response to questions
    How well did the speaker respond to questions from the group?
    Very well 1 2 3 4 5 Badly
    How?

17. Learner involvement
    To what extent were the learners involved in the session?
    A great deal 1 2 3 4 5 Not at all
    How appropriate was this level?

18. Classroom control
    How well did the teacher control the session and the learners?
    Effectively 1 2 3 4 5 Ineffectively
    In what way?

19. Handouts
    How adequate were the handouts?
    Adequate 1 2 3 4 5 Inadequate
    How?

20. Handouts 2
   How relevant were the handouts?
   Relevant 1 2 3 4 5 Not relevant
   Why?

21. Closing the session
   How well did the speaker bring the session to a close?
   Well 1 2 3 4 5 Badly
   What was the cause of this?

   Was a final summary used?

22. Timing
   How well did the speaker keep within the time constraints?
   Completely 1 2 3 4 5 Badly
   What were the principal causes?

23. Pace
   How well did the trainer pace the presentation?
   Very well 1 2 3 4 5 Badly
   How?

24. Appropriate approach
   Was this the most appropriate tactical approach for this subject or group?
   If not, what approach might be more appropriate?

25. Creativity
   To what extent was creativity of approach, methods, resources, etc. practised as required?
   Fully 1 2 3 4 5 Not at all
   In what circumstances?

26. Overall rating
   How would you rate the presentation of the session overall?
   Excellent 1 2 3 4 5 Poor

27. Any other comments

Appendix II

Discussion leading

Checklist

1. Opening platform presence
2. Opening of session
3. Sincerity
4. Enthusiasm
5. Setting the scene
6. Introducing the topic
7. Visual aids
8. Visual aids relevancy
9. Visual aids quality
10. Visual aids use
11. Discussion notes
12. Use of discussion notes
13. Use of questions
14. Types of question
15. Response to questions
16. Listening
17. Interventions
18. Value of interventions
19. Use of group
20. Bringing-in
21. Dealing with various members
22. Closing the session
23. Timing
24. Appropriate approach
25. Overall rating
26. Any other comments

TRAINER ASSESSMENT GUIDE

Discussion Leading

1. Opening platform presence
   To what extent did the trainer exhibit nervousness during the opening stages?
   None 1 2 3 4 5 A great deal
   How:

   How did this disappear as the session continued?
   Quickly 1 2 3 4 5 Not at all

2. Opening of session
   To what extent did the speaker obtain attention from the start?
   A great deal 1 2 3 4 5 Little
   How?

3. Sincerity
   How sincere and committed to the subject did the speaker appear to be?
   Very 1 2 3 4 5 Not at all
   What behaviours occurred?

4. Enthusiasm
   How enthusiastic was the speaker's manner?
   Very 1 2 3 4 5 Not at all
   In what way?

5. Setting the scene
   To what extent did the trainer prepare the discussion area before the start of the discussion?
   Well 1 2 3 4 5 Not at all
   How?

6. Introducing the topic
   How well did the trainer introduce the topic for discussion?
   Clearly 1 2 3 4 5 In a confused manner
   What happened?

7. Visual aids
   To what extent did the speaker use visual aids to vary the presentation?
   A great deal 1 2 3 4 5 Not at all

8. Visual aid relevancy
   To what extent were the visual aids, if used, relevant to the situation?
   Very 1 2 3 4 5 Not at all
   In what way?

9. Visual aids quality
   What was the quality of the visual aids used?
   Excellent 1 2 3 4 5 Poor
   How?

10. Visual aids use
    How effectively were the visual aids used?
    Very well 1 2 3 4 5 Badly
    How?

11. Discussion notes
Did the trainer have a prepared discussion note sheet/shopping list?
YES/NO

12. Use of discussion notes
If the trainer had discussion notes, how well were they used?
Unobtrusively 1 2 3 4 5 Obtrusively
In what way?

13. Use of questions
How well did the leader use questions to the group?
Very well 1 2 3 4 5 Badly
In what way?

14. Types of questions
Which types of questions did the leader use more than others? (place in descending order of use as far as possible)

OPEN	CLOSED
MULTIPLE	HYPOTHETICAL
LEADING	AGGRESSIVE
MULTI-CHOICE	REFLECTIVE
TESTING UNDERSTANDING	OTHERS

15. Response to questions
How well did the speaker respond to questions from the group?
Very well 1 2 3 4 5 Badly
How?

16. Listening
To what extent did the leader appear to listen when the group members were talking?
Fully 1 2 3 4 5 Not at all
What were the indications of this degree of listening?

17. Interventions
To what extent did the leader intervene in the discussion?
Rarely 1 2 3 4 5 Often

18. Value of interventions
When the leader intervened, were these interventions
Appropriate 1 2 3 4 5 Inappropriate
What types of intervention were used?

19. Use of group
To what extent did the leader bring in the quiet members?
A great deal 1 2 3 4 5 Not at all
What happened?

20. Bringing-in
How did the leader bring in the quiet members?
With skill 1 2 3 4 5 Clumsily
What happened?

21. Dealing with various members
     How well did the leader deal with difficult members?
     Well 1 2 3 4 5 Badly
     With what results?

22. Closing the discussion
     How well did the speaker bring the discussion to a close?
     Well 1 2 3 4 5 Badly
     What was done?

     Was a final summary used?

23. Timing
     How well did the speaker keep within the time constraints?
     Completely 1 2 3 4 5 Badly

24. Appropriate approach
     Was this the most appropriate tactical approach for this subject or group?

     If not, which approach might have been more appropriate?

25. Overall rating
     How would you rate the presentation of the session overall?
     Excellent 1 2 3 4 5 Poor

26. Any other comments

Appendix III

Activity control

Checklist

1. Opening of session
2. Sincerity
3. Enthusiasm
4. Setting the scene
5. Introducing the topic
6. Visual aids
7. Visual aids relevancy
8. Visual aids quality
9. Visual aids use
10. Activity description
11. Activity stages description
12. Activity briefs
13. Observers
14. Observer briefs
15. Trainer interventions
16. Activity feedback
17. Activity feedback (2)
18. Summary
19. Appropriateness of activity
20. Appropriateness of type of activity
21. Any other comments

TRAINER ASSESSMENT GUIDE

Activity control

1. Opening of session
   To what extent did the trainer obtain attention from the start?
   A great deal   1   2   3   4   5   Little
   How?

2. Sincerity
   How sincere and committed to the subject did the trainer appear to be?
   Very   1   2   3   4   5   Not at all
   How did this appear?

3. Enthusiasm
   How enthusiastic was the trainer's manner?
   Very   1   2   3   4   5   Not at all
   In what way?

4. Setting the scene
   To what extent did the trainer prepare the activity area(s) before the start of the discussion?
   Well   1   2   3   4   5   Not at all
   How?

5. Introducing the topic
   How well did the trainer introduce the activity?
   Clearly   1   2   3   4   5   In a confused manner
   What was the introduction?

6. Visual aids
   To what extent did the speaker use visual aids to introduce the activity?
   A great deal   1   2   3   4   5   None

7. Visual aids relevancy
   To what extent were the visual aids, if used, relevant to the situation?
   Very   1   2   3   4   5   Not at all
   Why?

8. Visual aids quality
   What was the quality of the visual aids used?
   Excellent   1   2   3   4   5   Poor
   In what way?

9. Visual aids use
   How effectively were the visual aids used?
   Very well   1   2   3   4   5   Badly
   What were the uses?

10. Activity description
    How clear was the trainer's description of the activity?
    Very clear   1   2   3   4   5   Not clear
    What was used?

11. Activity stages description
    How clear was the trainer's description of the stages of the activity?
    Very clear 1 2 3 4 5 Not clear
    How was this described?

12. Activity briefs
    How clear were the activity briefs issued to the participants?
    Very clear 1 2 3 4 5 Not clear
    In what way?

13. Observers
    How clear were the roles of the observers made?
    Very clear 1 2 3 4 5 Not clear
    Why?

14. Observer briefs
    How clear were the observers' briefs or observation forms?
    Very clear 1 2 3 4 5 Not clear
    How?

15. Trainer interventions
    To what extent did the trainer make appropriate interventions during the activity?
    Appropriately 1 2 3 4 5 Inappropriately
    What interventions were made?

16. Activity review
    How appropriate was the *method* of activity review?
    Very 1 2 3 4 5 Inappropriate
    Why?

17. Activity review 2
    How well did the trainer control the review?
    Very Well 1 2 3 4 5 Badly
    How?

18. Summary
    How well did the trainer summarize the lessons relating to the activity?
    Very well 1 2 3 4 5 Badly
    What happened?

19. Appropriateness of activity
    How appropriate was the activity in this event?
    Appropriate 1 2 3 4 5 Inappropriate
    Why was this so?

20. Appropriateness of type of activity
    How appropriate was the type of activity used?
    Appropriate 1 2 3 4 5 Inappropriate
    For what reasons?

21. Any other comments

Appendix IV

Practical demonstrations

Checklist

1. Introduction of subject
2. Description of object
3. Description of end result
4. Operation stages
5. Operation demonstration
6. Operating steps demonstration
7. Operting steps progression
8. Testing understanding
9. Questioning
10. Learner descriptions
11. Learner demonstrations
12. Appraisal of the learners
13. Learner control
14. Further practice
15. Overall performance
16. Relationship with co-trainer
17. Any other comments

TRAINER ASSESSMENT GUIDE

Practical Demonstrations

1. Introduction of subject
   How well were the objectives for the session presented?
   Very clearly   1   2   3   4   5   Unclearly
   How?

2. Description of object
   How well was the object described at the start of the sessions?
   Very well   1   2   3   4   5   Badly
   In what way?

3. Description of end result
   How well was the purpose of the object or the end result of its operation described
   at the start?
   Very well   1   2   3   4   5   Badly
   Why?

4. Operating stages
   How clearly were the operating stages described?
   Very clearly   1   2   3   4   5   Unclearly
   In what way?

5. Operation demonstration
   How well was the operation of the object demonstrated?
   Very well   1   2   3   4   5   Badly
   What happened?

6. Operating steps demonstration
   How clearly were the progressive operating steps demonstrated?
   Very clearly   1   2   3   4   5   Unclearly

7. Operating steps progression
   How well were the learners led through the practical steps of the session?
   Very well   1   2   3   4   5   Badly
   What happened?

8. Testing understanding
   To what extent did the trainer clarify understanding by asking questions?
   Extensively   1   2   3   4   5   Rarely
   What was done?

9. Questioning
   How appropriate were the types of questions in testing understanding?
   Appropriate   1   2   3   4   5   Inappropriate

10. Learner descriptions
    To what extent did the trainer require the learners to describe the object and its
    operation?
    Completely   1   2   3   4   5   Incompletely
    What happened?

11. Learner demonstrations
    To what extent did the trainer require the learners to demonstrate the operation of the object?
    Completely 1 2 3 4 5 Incompletely
    How?

12. Appraisal of the learners
    How effective was the trainer's appraisal of the learners' practical performance?
    Very effective 1 2 3 4 5 Ineffective

13. Learner control
    To what extent did the trainer recognize whether all the learners were with the trainer during the session.
    Completely 1 2 3 4 5 Not at all
    What happened?

14. Further practice
    What opportunities were given to the learners for further practice?
    Many 1 2 3 4 5 None
    In what way?

15. Overall performance
    How well did the trainer provide the demonstration?
    Very well 1 2 3 4 5 Badly

16. Relationship with co-trainer (if relevant)
    How well does the trainer relate to the co-trainer?
    To the appropriate extent 1 2 3 4 5 Not at all

17. Any other comments

Appendix V

Lecture, discussion leading and activity control sessions

Checklist

Common aspects
1. Opening platform presence
2. Opening of session
3. Continuation of session
4. Session objectives
5. Eye contact (showing interest)
6. Sincerity
7. Enthusiasm
8. General manner
9. Voice
10. Timing
11. Pace
12. Appropriate approach
13. Creativity
14. Use of group
15. Bringing-in
16. Dealing with various members

Lecture section
17. Visual aids
18. Visual aids relevance
19. Visual aids quality
20. Visual aids use
21. Subject coverage
22. Use of session notes
23. Response to questions
24. Handouts – adequacy
25. Handouts 2 – relevance
26. Pace

Discussion leading
27. Setting the scene
28. Introducing the topic
29. Discussion notes
30. Use of discussion notes
31. Use of questions
32. Types of question
33. Response to questions
34. Listening
35. Interventions
36. Value of interventions
37. Closing the discussion

Activity control
38. Setting the scene
39. Introducing the topic
40. Activity description
41. Activity stages description
42. Activity briefs
43. Observers
44. Observer briefs
45. Trainer interventions
46. Activity feedback
47. Activity feedback (2)
48. Summary
49. Appropriateness of activity
50. Appropriateness of type of activity

Final common aspects
51. Satisfaction of objectives
52. Overall performance
    During lecture
    During discussion section
    During activity section
53. Any other comments

LECTURE, DISCUSSION LEADING AND ACTIVITY CONTROL SESSIONS

Common aspects

1. Opening platform presence
    To what extent did the trainer exhibit nervousness during the opening stages?
    None 1 2 3 4 5 A great deal
    How?

    How did they disappear as the session continued?
    Quickly 1 2 3 4 5 Not at all

2. Opening of session
    To what extent did the speaker obtain attention from the start?
    A great deal 1 2 3 4 5 Little
    How?

3. Continuation of the session
   To what extent did the speaker maintain attention as the session progressed?
   All the time 1 2 3 4 5 Lost it
   How?

4. Session objectives
   How well were the objectives for the session introduced?
   Very well 1 2 3 4 5 Inadequately
   In what way?

5. Eye contact (showing interest)
   To what extent did the speaker maintain eye contact with the group?
   When Speaking
   Most of time 1 2 3 4 5 Rarely
   In which way?

   When Listening
   Most of time 1 2 3 4 5 Rarely
   In which way?

6. Sincerity
   How sincere and committed to the subject did the speaker appear to be?
   Very 1 2 3 4 5 Not at all
   How did this show?

7. Enthusiasm
   How enthusiastic was the speaker's manner?
   Very 1 2 3 4 5 Not at all
   How was this evidenced?

8. General manner
   To what extent did the speaker's manner relax you and encourage you to listen?
   A great deal 1 2 3 4 5 Little
   Which *distractive* mannerisms were present?

9. Voice
   How clear to the whole group was the speaker?
   Very clear 1 2 3 4 5 Unclear
   If unclear or tending towards unclear, in what way?

   How appropriate was the language used?
   Appropriate 1 2 3 4 5 Inappropriate

   If inappropriate or tending towards inappropriate, in what way?

10. Timing
    How well did the speaker keep within the time constraints?
    Completely 1 2 3 4 5 Badly
    What were the principal causes?

11. Pace
    How well did the trainer pace the complete session?
    Very well 1 2 3 4 5 Badly
    How?

12. Appropriate approach
    Was this the most appropriate tactical approach or this subject or group?

    If not, which approach might be more appropriate?

13. Creativity
    To what extent was creativity of approach, methods, resources, etc. practised as required?
    Fully 1 2 3 4 5 Not at all
    In what circumstances?

14. Use of group
    To what extent did the leader bring in the quiet members?
    A great deal 1 2 3 4 5 Not at all

15. Bringing-in
    How did the leader bring in the quiet members?
    With skill 1 2 3 4 5 Clumsily
    How?

16. Dealing with various members
    How well did the leader deal with difficult members?
    Well 1 2 3 4 5 Badly
    How?

Lecture Section
17. Visual aids
    To what extent did the speaker use visual aids to vary the presentation?
    A great deal 1 2 3 4 5 None
    In what way?

18. Visual aids relevance
    How relevant to the training were the visual aids?
    Relevant 1 2 3 4 5 Not relevant
    Why?

19. Visual aids quality
    What was the quality of the visual aids used?
    Excellent 1 2 3 4 5 Poor
    Why?

20. Visual aids use
    How effectively were the visual aids used?
    Very well 1 2 3 4 5 Badly
    How?

21. Subject coverage
    How well within the objectives was the subject covered?
    Completely 1 2 3 4 5 Poorly
    What was omitted or unclear?

22. Use of session notes
    Was the use of session notes distracting?
    Not at all 1 2 3 4 5 Very much
    In what way?

206

23. Response to questions
    How well did the speaker respond to questions from the group?
    Very well 1 2 3 4 5 Badly
    How?

24. Handouts
    How *adequate* were the handouts?
    Adequate 1 2 3 4 5 Inadequate
    How?

25. Handouts 2
    How *relevant* were the handouts?
    Relevant 1 2 3 4 5 Not relevant
    Why?

26. Pace
    How well did the trainer pace the presentation?
    Very well 1 2 3 4 5 Badly
    How?

Discussion leading
27. Setting the scene
    To what extent did the trainer prepare the discussion area before the start of the discussion?
    Well 1 2 3 4 5 Not at all
    In what way?

28. Introducing the topic
    How well did the trainer introduce the topic for discussion?
    Clearly 1 2 3 4 5 In a confused manner
    How?

29. Discussion notes
    Did the trainer have a prepared discussion note sheet/shopping list?
    Yes/No

30. Use of discussion notes
    If the trainer had discussion notes, how well were they used?
    Unobtrusively 1 2 3 4 5 Obtrusively
    How?

31. Use of questions
    How well did the leader use questions to the group?
    Very well 1 2 3 4 5 Badly
    In what way?

32. Types of question
    Which types of question did the leader use more than others (place in descending order of use as far as possible)

Open	Closed
Multiple	Hypothetical
Leading	Aggressive
Multi-choice	Reflective

Testing understanding   Others

33. Response to questions
How well did the speaker respond to questions from the group?
Very well 1 2 3 4 5 Badly
In what way?

34. Listening
To what extent did the leader appear to listen when the group members were talking?
Fully 1 2 3 4 5 Not at all
What were the indications of this extent of listening?

35. Interventions
To what extent did the leader intervene in the discussion?
Rarely 1 2 3 4 5 Often

36. Value of intervention
When the leader intervened, were these interventions
Appropriate 1 2 3 4 5 Inappropriate
In what way?

37. Closing the discussion
How well did the speaker bring the discussion to a close?
Well 1 2 3 4 5 Badly
In what way?

Was a final summary used?

Activity
38. Setting the scene
To what extent did the trainer prepare the activity area(s) before the start of the discussion?
Well 1 2 3 4 5 Not at all
How?

39. Introducing the topic
How well did the trainer introduce the activity?
Clearly 1 2 3 4 5 In a confused manner
How?

40. Activity description
How clear was the trainer's description of the activity?
Very clear 1 2 3 4 5 Not clear
In what way?

41. Activity stages description
How clear was the trainer's description of the stages of the activity?
Very clear 1 2 3 4 5 Not clear
In what way?

42. Activity briefs
How clear were the activity briefs issued to the participants?
Very clear 1 2 3 4 5 Not clear
How?

43. Observers
How clear were the roles of the observers made?
Very clear 1 2 3 4 5 Not clear
In what way?

44. Observer briefs
How clear were the observers' briefs or observation forms?
Very clear 1 2 3 4 5 Not clear
How?

45. Trainer intervention
To what extent did the trainer make appropriate interventions during the activity?
Appropriately 1 2 3 4 5 Inappropriately
In what way?

46. Activity review
How appropriate was the *method* of activity review?
Very 1 2 3 4 5 Inappropriate
In what way?

47. Activity review 2
How well did the trainer control the review?
Very Well 1 2 3 4 5 Badly
In what way?

48. Summary
How well did the trainer summarize the lessons relating to the activity?
Very well 1 2 3 4 5 Badly
How?

49. Appropriateness of activity?
How appropriate was the activity in this event?
Appropriate 1 2 3 4 5 Inappropriate
Why?

50. Appropriateness of type of activity
How appropriate was the type of activity used?
Appropriate 1 2 3 4 5 Inappropriate
Why?

51. Satisfaction of objectives
To what extent were the session objectives satisfied?
Completely 1 2 3 4 5 Not at all
Why?

52. Overall performance
How well did the trainer perform during the lecture section?
Very well 1 2 3 4 5 Badly

How well did the trainer perform during the discussion section?
Very well 1 2 3 4 5 Badly

How well did the trainer perform during the activity section?
Very well 1 2 3 4 5 Badly

Any additional reasons other than those referred to in previous parts?

53. Any other comments

Appendix VI

Assessment of trainer by trainee

TRAINER ASSESSMENT

COURSE ....

Please complete the following questions by placing a tick or other mark against each question under the heading that most nearly represents your view.

It will help the trainer and his/her manager in the trainer's development if you would complete the questionnaire fully and honestly. There is no intention to use it in any way as a discipline document and it will support other assessments of the trainer's effectivenmess.

		To a large extent	Partly	Hardly at all
1.	To what extent did he create interest from the start?	....	....	....
2.	How much did he maintain this interest?	....	....	....
3.	To what extent did he declare the objectives of the course?	....	....	....
4.	To what extent did he just *tell* you?	....	....	....
5.	How much did he involve the group?	....	....	....
6.	How much did he use visual/audio aids?	....	....	....
7.	Were the aids of good quality?	....	....	....
8.	Were the aids revelant?	....	....	....
9.	How much variety was there in the course?	....	....	....

10. How much use of summaries did he make? ....

11. To what extent was the language used understandable? ....

12. How much enthusiasm did he show? ....

13. To what extent did he listen to the group? ....

14. How much opportunity was the group given to pose questions? ....

15. How much did his 'platform presence' distract you? ....

16. To what extent was he responsible for what you learned? ....

17. Any other comments. ....

Recommended reading

There are few publications dealing specifically with this subject, mainly because most of the assessment emphasis so far has been on the examination of *training* rather than the *trainer*.

Bennett, R. (Ed.) (1988) *Improving Trainer Effectiveness*. Gower.

Bennett, R. (1983) 'The effective trainer', *Journal of the Institute of Training and Development*, 3, 4.

Bennett, R. and Leduchowicz, T. (1983), 'What makes for an effective trainer', *Journal of European Industrial Training Monograph*, 7 (2).

Jones, J. A. G. (1982) 'Making training interventions more effective', *Journal of European Industrial Training*, 6 (6).

Jones, J. A. G. (1983) 'Training intervention strategies', *Journal of the Institute of Training and Development*, 3 (5).

Leduchowicz, T. (1982) 'Trainer role and effectiveness – a review of the literature', *International Journal of Manpower*, 3 (i).

Pettigrew, A. M., Jones, G. R. and Reason, P. W. (1983) 'Training and developmental roles in their organisational setting', *Journal of the Institute of Training and Development*, 3 (6).

Rae, L. (1991) *The Skills of Training* (2nd edn). Gower.

Rae, L. (1986, 2nd edn, 1991) *How to Measure Training Effectiveness*. Gower.

MSC/ITD, (1984) *Guide to Trainer Effectiveness*.

MSC/ITD, (1984) *Trainer Task Inventory*.

Index